OM YOGA TODAY

OM YOGA TODAY

YOUR YOGA PRACTICE IN 5, 15, 30, 60, AND 90 MINUTES

Written and Illustrated by Cyndi Lee

Concept and Design by Laurie Dolphin

CHRONICLE BOOKS

SAN FRANCISCO

Acknowledgments:
Thank you! Thank you! Thank you! to my funny, wildly creative, and kind partner, Laurie Dolphin. Much gratitude to our generous and supportive editor, Sarah Malarkey. Thanks to my parents for teaching me the right ways to spend my time and to my husband for spending so much time talking about yoga.

Library of Congress Cataloging-in-Publication Data available.

ISBN: 0-8118-4446-3

Manufactured in China

Designed by Laurie Dolphin Design

Distributed in Canada by Raincoast Books
9050 Shaughnessy Street
Vancouver, British Columbia V6P 6E5

10 9 8 7 6 5 4 3 2 1

Chronicle Books LLC
85 Second Street
San Francisco, California 94105

www.chroniclebooks.com

Not all exercises are suitable for everyone. Your physical condition and health are important factors in determining which yoga exercises, positions, and advice may be appropriate. This or any other exercise program may result in injury. The packager, author, and publisher of this book disclaim any liability from any injury that may result from the use, proper or improper, of any exercise or advice contained in this book. Please consult your professional health care provider for information and advice on the suitability of your exercise program.

Contents

Stretching Time

How often do you feel that you just do not have enough time in the day? The condition of having too little time has practically become an epidemic among my group of friends. We rush in late to meet for dinner with each other and are relieved when we don't have to feel guilty, because the other person arrives even later. We all tend to be stressed about how much activity we cram into a day, then waste even more time comparing notes about the demands on our time. We come to the conclusion that there never seems to be enough time.

Why do we all seem to have less and less time? In our society, empty time and open space are not considered advantages. Everything is getting faster and more compressed. On television and radio, even in our ordinary conversations, one of the worst things that can happen is a moment of silence. In fact, silence is so rare that it has taken on special meaning, as in "Let's take a moment of silence to reflect on and pay homage to someone who is gone." This kind of density creates a sense of pressure and claustrophobia for many of us, as well as a need to push harder, to accomplish more, before time runs out.

My observation is that there is a direct relationship that goes like this:

thinking about what has to happen in the future = less time now
moving slowly and mindfully now = more time now

As a yoga teacher, I have the frequent delight of people telling me about their positive yoga experiences. I also hear plenty of reasons why people want to do yoga but just can't find the time. Where did that time go? How did we lose it? Let's face it: the time is still there, but it is filled with other things. My Buddhist teacher, Gelek Rinpoche, often says there are two kinds of laziness: Eastern laziness, which takes the form of people sitting on a cushion with a cup of tea all day, and Western laziness, which is people being way too busy all the time.

So for many of us, even if we have the good intention to begin practicing yoga, the first obstacle is finding the time. But here's some good news: yoga is a great multitasking activity for us busy types because you get a physical workout, meditation, cardiovascular enhancement, and emotional processing all in one. On top of that, the practice of yoga somehow creates time. I cannot prove this scientifically, but I know it's true.

For one thing, yoga falls into the categories of both short-term and long-term plans. Fairly quickly, you will find that—unlike with other forms of physical exercise, where you generally need to work out a couple of times a week to get anywhere—even if you do yoga only once a week, you will soon begin to experience tangible benefits, such as better sleep, improved digestion, stronger muscles and bones, increased energy, and a healthy sense of physical confidence. This is the short-term aspect of yoga, and for those of us who don't have a lot of extra time, it's encouraging to know that we can see palpable results in the first few months—maybe even sooner.

But eventually many people become aware that it's not just the physical boons that keep them coming back to yoga practice. There is a deeper layer to yoga, one related to its long-term aspect. This shows up when we start getting curious about the process or the experiences that arise during our yoga practice, rather than just trying to put a check mark next to the words "yoga practice" written on our agenda for that day. Being part of a process creates a different sense of time from that of wanting to complete a project. Our question shifts from "How much can I accomplish in this amount of time?" to "How can I open into this experience?"

This doesn't mean that there is no real purpose to doing yoga or that there can be no meaningful results. The process of getting quiet, letting go of external demands, becoming sensuous, slowing down, and relaxing our agenda is the path to cultivating curiosity, groundedness, clarity, patience, compassion, kindness, relaxed alertness, and a sense of well-being. These qualities, which you will probably start to experience even in just five minutes, will begin to leak out into the rest of your life, providing an antidote to anxiety, habitual rushing, and all the pressure-cooker situations of your work, family, society, and world. This is how yoga creates time, spaciousness, and a sense of possibility, not only in your schedule but in all of your relationships.

Well-known yoga teacher Judith Lasater likes to point out that we all have the same amount of time in a day. Some of us might have more stuff we want to squish into our calendars, but we each

have the same allotment of twenty-four hours daily. This book is about how to develop a yoga practice within the wide variety of twenty-four-hour days in your ever-changing life. When you are on vacation, you might do a ninety-minute practice, and when you are in a dense work period, you can slip in a five-minute practice right in your office.

So the good news is that you don't have to change anything in order to practice yoga. Not even your schedule. This is the invitation that yoga extends to us, and we don't need to make a big deal out of it. Many people think that in order to do yoga they may have to change their religion, their dress, their diet, their friends, or their busy schedule. But yoga is flexible and fluid and can fit into any person's life and schedule.

Somehow yoga finds time for itself. If it seems like just one more thing to do, start with only five minutes, but start. The increased sense of spaciousness in your life, your relationships, and your habits happens naturally from the doing, not from the planning to do it. It is a result of the practice of yoga, not the cause.

It is possible that yoga will change your life—you might give up all worldly activities and move into an ashram and become celibate. But you might not. It's quite likely, though, that you will find that you have better concentration in conversations with your loved ones, more patience in traffic, more energy available for what is important to you right now. This is how yoga changes your life, and it happens minute by minute, breath by breath.

You can start right now.

How to Use This Book

In order to help you find the time for your yoga practice, this book offers five different sequences created for the kind of time bites most of us use to measure our activities: five minutes, fifteen minutes, thirty minutes, sixty minutes, and ninety minutes. Each session builds on the sequences of the prior sessions. For instance, the Thirty-Minute Session incorporates the sun salutations covered in the Fifteen-Minute Session. All the sequences are shown flowed together on the opening pages of each section. The pages following give directions on how to do each pose. Some sequences, such as the Warm-Up Vinyasa, are explained in the earlier sessions only. The book then refers you back to these pages, should you need more explanation in the later sections.

Every one of the time frames contains a full yoga practice involving the following elements in a flowing sequence that connects breath and movement:

forward bending • twisting • backward bending • side bending • balancing • inverting • breath awareness • resting • meditation

Choose the time you have today. If you haven't done yoga before, start with five minutes. If you are feeling busy, start with five minutes. If you are thinking, "I know this is good for me, but I really would rather lie down on the couch with a juicy mystery and some ice cream," choose five minutes. If, by some wonderful twist of fate, you have the house cleaned or your desk cleared and you still have fifteen minutes until your kids come home or until your next appointment, there is a fifteen-minute sequence waiting for you. You get the idea.

You can choose according to the actual amount of time open to you, or according to your resistance to doing yoga at all. Something is always better than nothing, so please just bite off what you feel you can chew today.

If you find that your time begins to expand as you get involved in your yoga practice, feel free to take longer with any of these elements. You can repeat sequences, but try to work with the material in the progression that it is given, in order to get the most benefit from each practice.

How to Meditate

Meditation has sometimes been described as a "gathering of energy." Many of us tend to unconsciously disperse our energy by trying to do too many things at once. When we practice meditation, we are practicing doing one thing at a time. That thing is simply sitting still while paying attention to what is happening in your mind. It is not an attempt to remove all thoughts from your mind. It is natural for thoughts to arise in your mind—how else could we function in the world? But often we do not have an awareness of our thoughts or any sense of separation between what we are thinking and what is actually happening. It is not unusual to sit perfectly still, doing nothing with your body, but meanwhile your mind is far away, involved in some other activity, such as making dinner, going on a date, shopping, or planning a presentation. Sound familiar?

Meditation is a simple technique for harmonizing your body and mind—in other words, for learning how to do one thing at a time. This will help you cultivate focus, concentration, presence of mind, and, over time, a greater sense of composure and confidence. When we have more energy at our fingertips instead of dispersed all over the place, we can experience our lives more fully. This is another way of creating time, because when you are present, you don't lose time.

I recommend beginning and/or ending your yoga session with a short sitting meditation. Starting off your practice with meditation can give you a wonderful sense of grounding and presence. You may also discover that it feels natural and inviting to meditate at the end of your yoga session. Either way or both is fine. Feel free to experiment for yourself. It is great if you can meditate every day, even when you're not doing yoga. You will discover that even five minutes is a worthwhile and of course, you can always sit for longer if you like.

Here's how to do it:

* Sit on the floor or in a chair. If you sit on the floor, you will most likely need to use a cushion or two in order to be perched right on your sitting bones. This is important, because if your pelvis is tucked under, it will strain your back muscles. Find a point of comfort and balance so that your spine is naturally lifted. If you are sitting on a chair, sit on the front edge of the chair to avoid slumping and falling asleep.

* Place your palms on your thighs in the hand position called "calm abiding." Keep your eyes open about halfway and let your gaze rest on the floor roughly four feet in front of you. Try not to let your focus go fuzzy; at the same time, let the muscles around your eyes stay soft—in focus but not staring.

* Begin to notice the movement of your breath. Let your breathing pattern remain natural. Follow the breath in and out. When you notice that your mind has strayed from your breath and that you have gotten involved in a train of thought, gently return your attention to your breath. This will happen over and over, and that's fine. This is a process with no end or beginning.

* Remember, we are not trying to remove thoughts. We are developing awareness of when we get lost in thoughts, and we are also practicing letting go. Even if you have an incredibly brilliant idea, release it and return to your breath. If it's a really good idea, you will remember it later, so don't worry about having to grab it right now. There are so many things we are trying to hold on to, and this grasping tendency is similar to doing too many things at the same time. These are some of the ways we disperse our energy. Meditation is a technique for letting go of all those distractions and coming back to where we are right now, over and over and over.

If you don't have time to sit down and meditate, you can incorporate a sense of meditative aware-ness into your daily life as you walk from place to place—even from the couch to the refrigerator and back! Slow down your pace slightly and begin to be sensitive to the feeling of each footfall. Since you are traveling through space, it is important that you remain mindful and alert to the world around you, but still it is amazing how much our minds zone out even when we are walking or driv-ing. When you recognize that your mind has drifted off in thought, use the sensation of your feet on the earth as the home base for returning your mind to the present.

Breathing and Moving

The connection between mind and body is the breath. We can use the breath as a reference point for resting in the present moment when we are moving our bodies, similar to the technique for mindfulness during meditation.

In yoga practice, both the inhalation and exhalation are done through the nose. Sit on a cushion or a chair, close your eyes, and watch your breath. Instead of using the breath as a reference point for the present moment, this time we will explore the breath as a way of understanding ourselves. As you observe your breath, you may wish to consider these inquiries:

* Am I holding my breath?

* Am I breathing fast, slow, hard, soft?

* Can I feel my breath in my lower abdomen? Middle abdomen? Chest?

* Can I imagine my breath moving throughout my body—under my armpits, between my toes, along the back of my neck, through the inside of my knees?

* Is there any difference between me and my breath?

Practice observing your breath in this way for a few minutes.

Calming Breath

Equalizing the length and quality of the inhalation and exhalation is a way to balance your active and receptive aspects. Choose any length of time—four counts is a good place to start—and breathe in and out evenly for that duration. Notice what effect this has on your nervous system.

In meditation, we let our breathing remain natural, but as you begin your yoga practice your breathing patterns will change according to what you are doing and how you feel about it. Work on cultivating a smooth breath in and out your nose during your yoga practice, but don't worry about it if your breath varies from time to time. When you turn upside down and inside out, that's bound to happen. See if you can let your breath begin the movements between each pose. Explore the possibility of letting the movement and the breath be the same thing.

Pay attention to your breath in a way similar to what you did in your meditation, but with a lighter touch, so that it becomes part of the entire panorama of sensation, inside and outside you. You will probably begin to notice that everything affects the breath—your emotions, your physical effort, your eating and drinking habits, your environment. Continue to ask questions, observe, and relax. After all, it's just you and your breath.

We can go without food for weeks and water for a few days, but how long can we go without breath? This profound life essence is something we often don't even notice. Now is a good time to begin to cultivate breath awareness.

What Is OM?

OM is said to be the sound of the universe. Everything in the universe moves in cycles, and this oscillating activity creates a pulse, a hum. If you close your eyes and listen very carefully, you can hear your own heartbeat. If you stand very still, you will begin to notice that you are swaying in an organic response to the rotation of the earth.

The recognition of these life rhythms is how time was first measured, and how it is still measured, in its most profound meaning. Birth and death, day and night, the cycle of the seasons, the ebb and flow of the tides, the phases of the moon—these are all ways we experience the passing of time.

When we chant "OM," it is a way to sound the wavelike energies of our heartbeats, breathing, emotions, and thoughts as they are happening right in this moment. You can hear the quality of your own energy today—maybe you are loose, maybe you are tight, maybe you are flowing, or maybe you feel somewhat blocked. It doesn't matter. What you hear is not important; it's the listening that we are cultivating. Listening to your own genuine sounding of OM is like looking in the mirror—it's a way to learn something about yourself. Without judging or wishing anything were different, we can simply listen with close attention to our OMs. Let each OM be a reminder that your rhythm is also part of the universal timepiece.

OM is also a traditional way to begin and end a yoga class. Take a deep breath, and as you exhale, make the sound "ooooooommmmm." Chant OM three times. Let your OM be a vocal framing of this time set aside just for you to connect inward to your own heart and mind, as well as outward to the rhythm of the whole world.

Five-Minute Session

Beloved meditation teacher Dipa Ma had many householder meditation students (that is, meditation practitioners who have a home, job, and family). When one very active businesswoman and mother said she didn't have time to practice meditation, Dipa Ma sat down with her right then and there, and they had a brief meditation session together on the spot. Then Dipa Ma advised her simply to begin with five minutes a day. The woman reported that after meeting Dipa Ma she somehow managed to find that small stretch of time after all, and the positive experience of those five minutes evolved effortlessly into longer and longer periods of practice.

For almost everyone, the thought of an hour-and-a-half yoga session is daunting, not to mention time-consuming. But how about five minutes? This five-minute session is a soothing sequence of poses that will stimulate your circulation and relax your muscles. Think of how many things you do that take five minutes, and how many of them—such as gossiping, reviewing the contents of the refrigerator, looking in the mirror—you don't need to do today, or ever again.

I can almost guarantee that once you do this yoga program a few times it will become less difficult for you to find a spare five-minute slot. If you still don't think you have five minutes, just pick one of the things on the list of yoga elements, and do that for five breaths. (Hey, you can even do the last two in bed!) Later in the day, do another one. By the end of the day you will have done a complete yoga program. Who knows? Maybe those five breaths will evolve into ten breaths, which is about one minute, and then that one minute will turn into five. Only time will tell.

Five-Minute Session

1 calming breath:
three inhales/exhales

2 downward dog:
six breaths

3 hand walking
meditation

4 standing
forward bend

5 standing cat

6 standing cow:
do cat/cow three times

7 standing side bend:
three breaths each side

8 knee into chest

9 chair pose

10 locust pose

11 supine spinal twist

12 corpse pose

calming breath: three inhales/exhales

Breathe evenly, in and out, through your nose. Choose whatever length of inhale and exhale is comfortable for you today.

downward dog

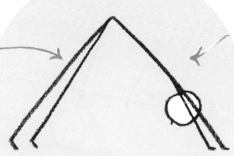

Keep leg muscles strong.

Create length in your spine by reaching pelvis away from hands.

Hold for three to five breaths.

Your belly can be soft to allow for free breathing.

hand walking meditation

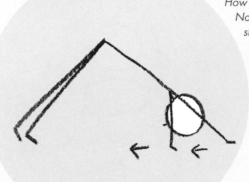

How sensitive can you be?
Notice the gradual
shifting of weight from
four things to two things,
the texture of your mat
under your hands,
the subtle changes
in your breath. See
everything along the way.

Starting from downward
dog, slowly walk your hands
back to your feet. It's OK to
bend your knees at any time.

3

standing forward bend

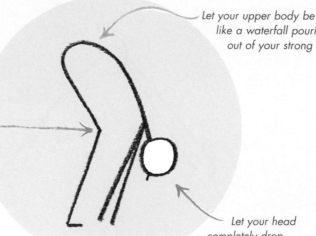

Let your upper body be
like a waterfall pouring
out of your strong legs.

Bend your knees
if you are tight
anywhere in back,
including the back
of your legs. If not,
you can straighten
your knees.

Let your head
completely drop.

4

standing cat: three times

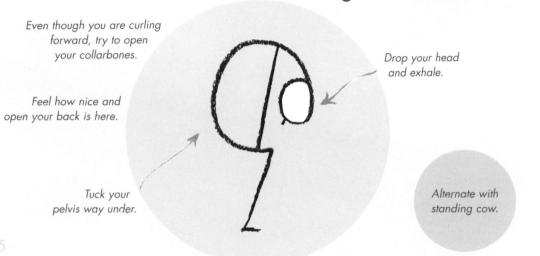

Even though you are curling forward, try to open your collarbones.

Feel how nice and open your back is here.

Tuck your pelvis way under.

Drop your head and exhale.

Alternate with standing cow.

5

standing cow: three times

Arch your back. Make your sitting bones flare open.

Inhale fully.

Look up.

6

standing side bend

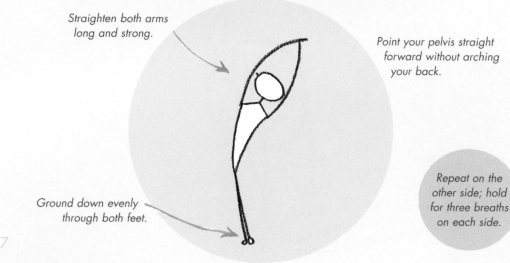

Straighten both arms long and strong.

Point your pelvis straight forward without arching your back.

Ground down evenly through both feet.

Repeat on the other side; hold for three breaths on each side.

7

knee into chest

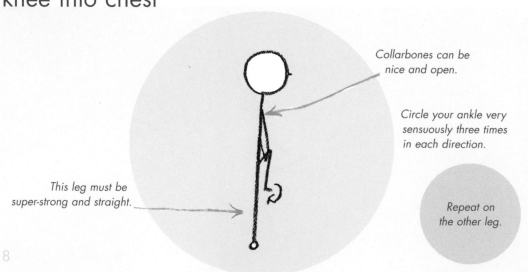

Collarbones can be nice and open.

Circle your ankle very sensuously three times in each direction.

This leg must be super-strong and straight.

Repeat on the other leg.

8

chair pose

Lightly engage your abdominal muscles.

Press your palms together to remind you of your midline.

If you feel like you are leaning forward, make sure your thighs are parallel to the floor, which will lift your spine.

Explore how to sit on your heels without dropping your entire weight onto your feet. (Hint! Squeeze your legs together!)

Hold for two to three breaths.

9

locust pose

Your feet can be as wide apart as your hips.

Breathe with the back of the neck.

Think of touching the wall behind you with your toes.

Lift from the sternum and the heart.

Can you engage your buttocks without gripping them?

Hold for three breaths.

10

supine spinal twist ✓

Relax your neck
and throat.

It's OK if you can't stack
the top knee directly over
the bottom one.

Release your weight
into the floor.

Hold for three
breaths and then
switch to the
other side.

Turn the palms up.

11

corpse pose

You can
also simply
lie down flat
on the ground
and rest.

Feet should be about
hip distance apart.

Close your eyes.
An eye pillow
can be nice.

Stay here as long
as you like.

A pillow under your
knees can feel good
to your lower back.

Turn your palms up.

12

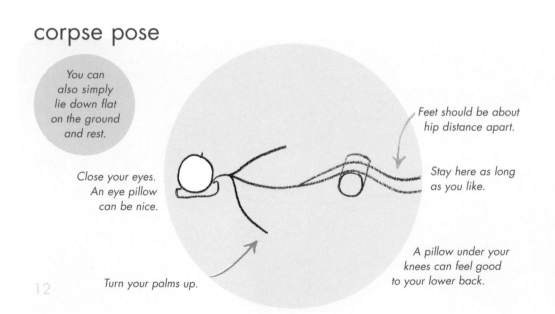

Daily Relaxation

The relaxation pose that completes each yoga session is a traditional element considered to be one of the most important parts of our yoga practice. This is when the physical benefits of the postures get a chance to absorb deeply into your nervous system.

I know what you're thinking—who has time to relax? And, certainly not every day. But when you are able to release your outgoing efforts, even for a few minutes, you may find out a lot about yourself. This information is a very important step toward experiencing balance in your life. For example, you may actually find out that it is hard for you to let go. You may find out that your mind is very active. Or you may fall asleep immediately and discover that you are even more exhausted than you thought. It is said that the relaxation that comes from this time of letting go is more restorative than sleeping. When you sleep you toss and turn, have vibrant dreams, negotiate the blanket with another person—who might even be snoring! The quality of relaxation after doing yoga practice is so yummy that once you experience it you will know how valuable it is.

Try to make a commitment to doing at least a few minutes of daily relaxation every time you practice your yoga. This brief time of letting go, of resting, of not doing anything at all, will truly be time well spent.

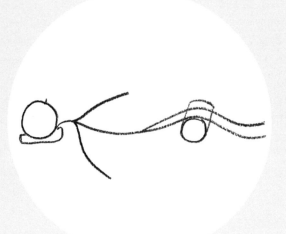

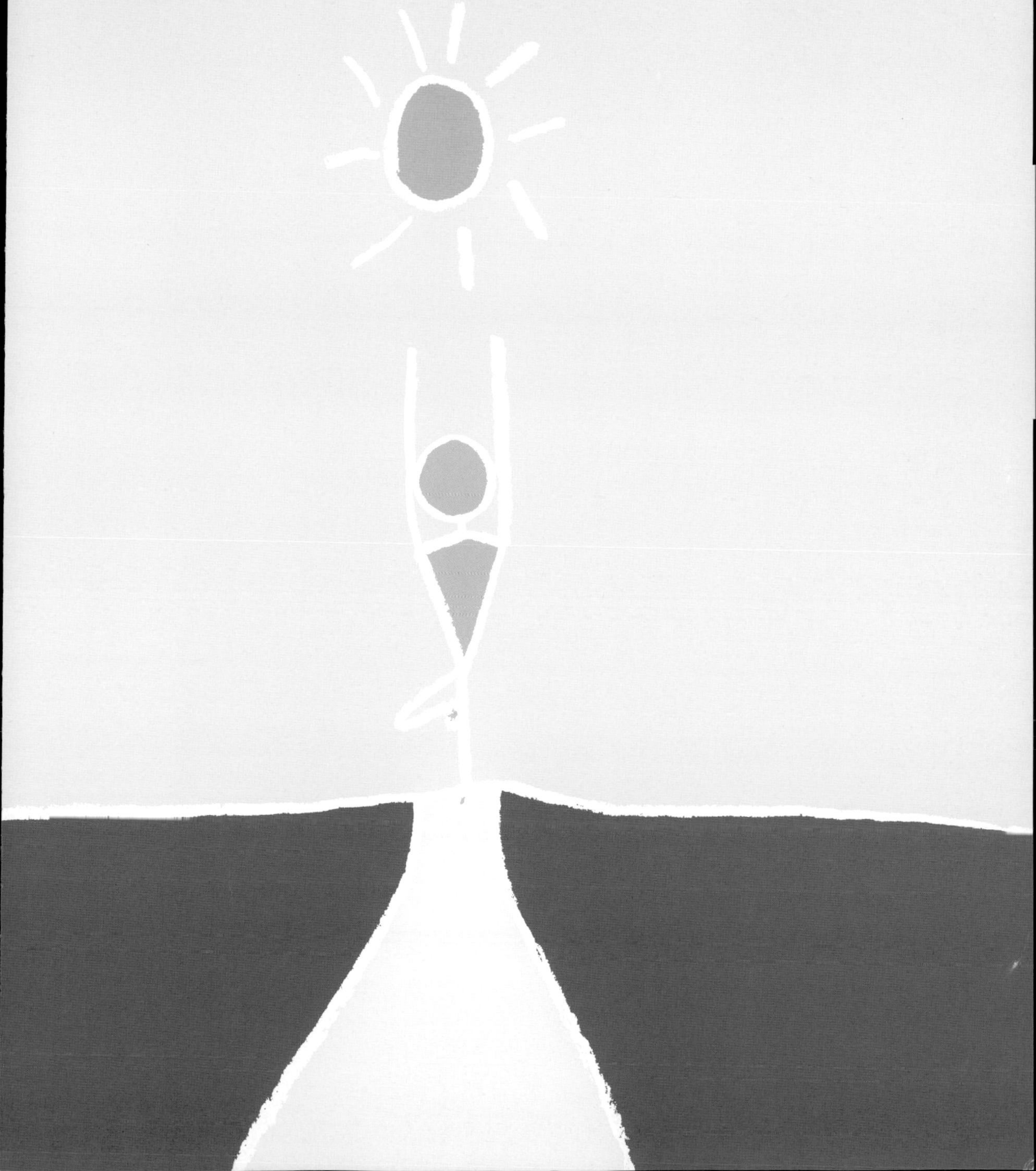

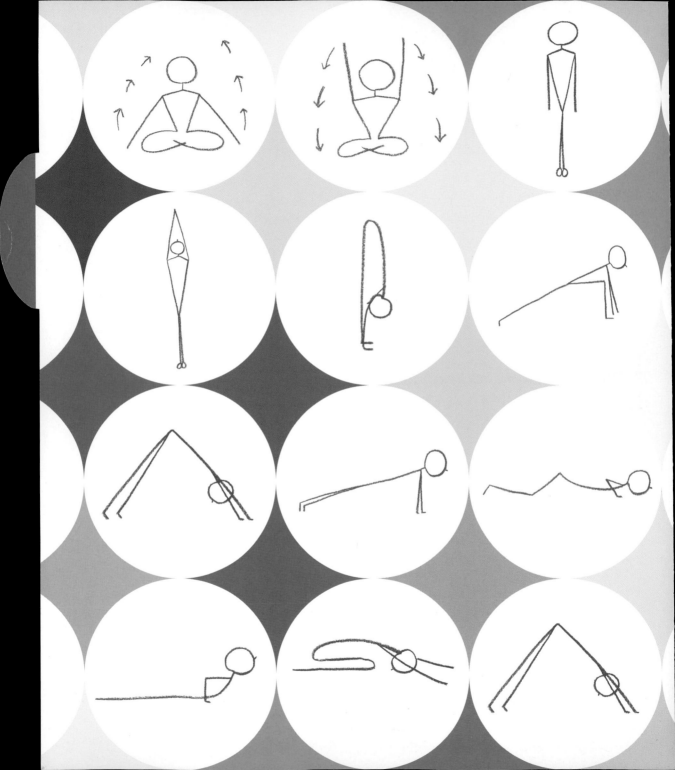

Fifteen-Minute Session

Recently I walked into one of the four yoga classrooms at my studio, OM Yoga Center in New York City, to attend an evening yoga class. The space was full of yogis and yoginis, and I was delighted to see that more and more people are discovering yoga. As we waited for the teacher to begin the class, I observed the different energies of the students. It was obvious that some of the folks there enjoyed being in a room with many like-minded people, finding the group energy uplifting and fun. Others were quietly doing their own thing, undisturbed, in their own private places on their yoga mats. But some folks were made uncomfortable by the number of people in the room. It was clear that they felt spatially compromised and downright annoyed.

Our teacher, Margi, began the class by welcoming all of us and then acknowledging that we had a full house that night. She suggested that although it might be irritating to some of us at first, she was pretty sure that our feelings would shift as we began to connect to our breathing and our bodies. Margi cheerfully invited us to "just wait for fifteen minutes and see if you still feel annoyed." Fifteen minutes came and went. By that time, the entire space had been transformed as we all began to relax our edges, focus inward, get grounded, let go of conceptual thinking, and be more attuned to sensation. The number of people in the room was the same, but the space in our minds had expanded.

At OM we like to say "before yoga and after yoga."

Aren't you curious to see what can happen in only fifteen minutes? The fifteen-minute sequence builds on the five-minute sequence, introduces sun salutations, and ends with a soothing relaxation pose.

Fifteen-Minute Session

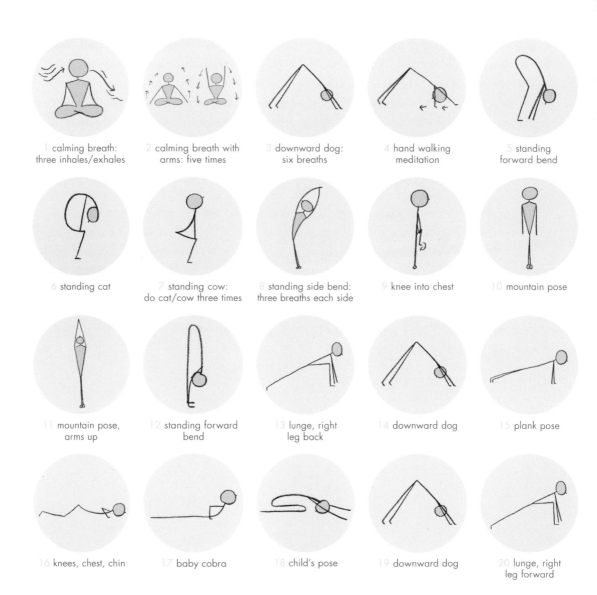

1 calming breath: three inhales/exhales

2 calming breath with arms: five times

3 downward dog: six breaths

4 hand walking meditation

5 standing forward bend

6 standing cat

7 standing cow: do cat/cow three times

8 standing side bend: three breaths each side

9 knee into chest

10 mountain pose

11 mountain pose, arms up

12 standing forward bend

13 lunge, right leg back

14 downward dog

15 plank pose

16 knees, chest, chin

17 baby cobra

18 child's pose

19 downward dog

20 lunge, right leg forward

21 standing forward bend

22 mountain pose, arms up

23 mountain pose

Repeat poses 10–23: beginning with left leg; then repeat again on both sides.

24 mountain pose

25 mountain pose, arms up

26 standing forward bend

27 lunge, right leg back

28 downward dog

29 plank pose

30 knees, chest, chin

31 baby cobra

32 child's pose

33 downward dog

34 lunge, right leg forward

35 warrior one

36 warrior two

37 cartwheel

38 lunge, right leg forward

39 downward dog

Fifteen-Minute Session

40 lunge, left
leg forward

41 warrior one

42 warrior two

43 cartwheel

44 lunge, left
leg forward

45 downward dog

46 plank pose

47 knees, chest, chin

48 baby cobra

49 child's pose

50 downward dog

51 lunge, right
leg forward

52 standing forward
bend

53 powerful pose

54 mountain pose,
arms up

55 mountain pose
with prayer hands

Repeat poses
24–55, beginning
with left leg; then
repeat again on
both sides.

56 tree pose

57 cobbler's pose

58 seated spinal twist

59 half wheel

60 legs up the wall

61 corpse pose

calming breath: three inhales/exhales

Breathe evenly, in and out, through your nose. Choose whatever length of inhale and exhale is comfortable for you today.

Try to hold this pose for three to five breaths.

1

calming breath with arms: five times

2*

Inhale evenly, drawing your breath down as your arms float all the way up next to your ears.

Exhale smoothly, keeping the spine lifted as the arms lower down to the floor.

*For poses 3–9, see pages 17–20

mountain pose

Let the softness of your front invite you to be open to whatever arises.

Bring your feet together and feel your weight dropping to the earth.

Hold for three breaths.

mountain pose, arms up

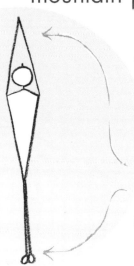

Look up and see your palms meeting.

Press your palms together by using your arm muscles.

Inhale.

As you reach your arms up, reach your feet down, so that your whole body lengthens in two directions.

standing forward bend

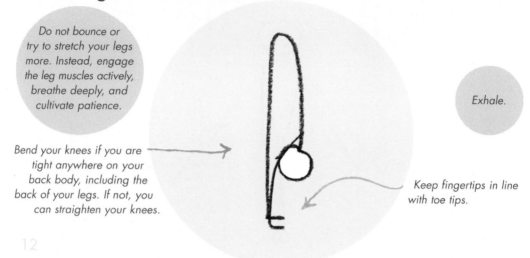

Do not bounce or try to stretch your legs more. Instead, engage the leg muscles actively, breathe deeply, and cultivate patience.

Exhale.

Bend your knees if you are tight anywhere on your back body, including the back of your legs. If not, you can straighten your knees.

Keep fingertips in line with toe tips.

12

lunge, right leg back

Spine stays long.

Keep your chest open.

Reach through your back heel so that back leg is long.

Inhale.

13

downward dog

Keep leg muscles strong.

Create length in your spine by reaching pelvis away from hands.

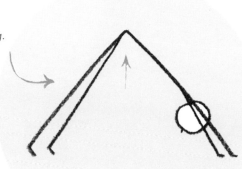

Your belly can be soft to allow for free breathing.

Exhale.

plank pose

Slightly tone your belly to support the spine.

Inhale.

Extend energy out through your heels.

Keep arms and legs straight.

Keep wrists below your shoulders.

knees, chest, chin

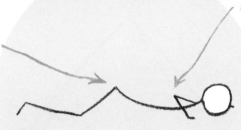

Sitting bones spin upward.

Keep elbows tight into your ribs and your palms flat on the floor.

Lower your knees, chest, and chin to the floor.

Exhale.

16

baby cobra

Lengthen your legs.

Keep your neck long.

Elbows stay close to the body.

Point your toes.

Bottom ribs touch the floor.

Slide the hips forward to lift the chest.

Inhale.

17

child's pose

Drop your hips all the way back onto your heels.

Feel your deep, full breath moving your back muscles.

Exhale.

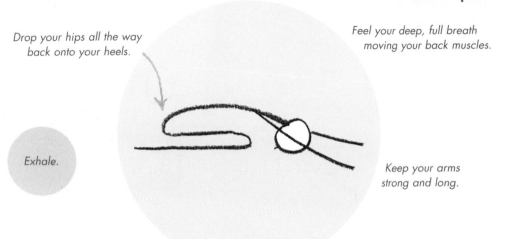

Keep your arms strong and long.

downward dog

Hold this downward-facing dog for three to five breaths. A breath means one complete inhale and exhale.

Create length in your spine by reaching pelvis away from hands.

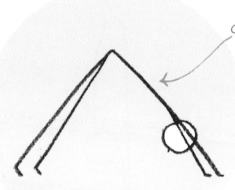

lunge, right leg forward

Spine stays long.

Inhale.

Step your right foot all the way up between your hands. You can use your right hand to adjust it forward if you need to.

20

standing forward bend

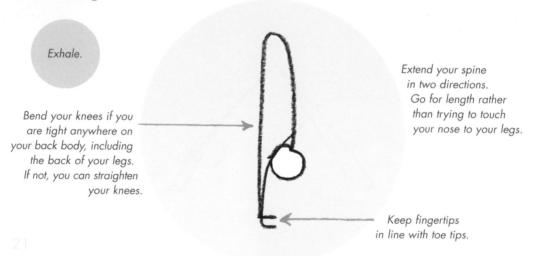

Exhale.

Bend your knees if you are tight anywhere on your back body, including the back of your legs. If not, you can straighten your knees.

Extend your spine in two directions. Go for length rather than trying to touch your nose to your legs.

Keep fingertips in line with toe tips.

21

mountain pose, arms up

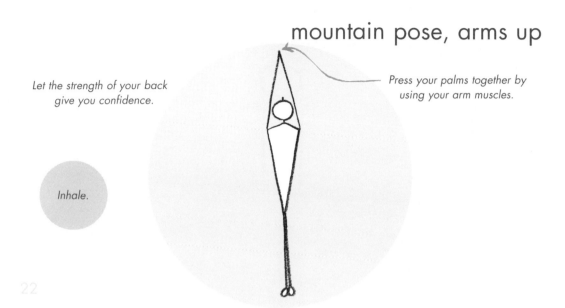

Let the strength of your back give you confidence.

Press your palms together by using your arm muscles.

Inhale.

22

mountain pose

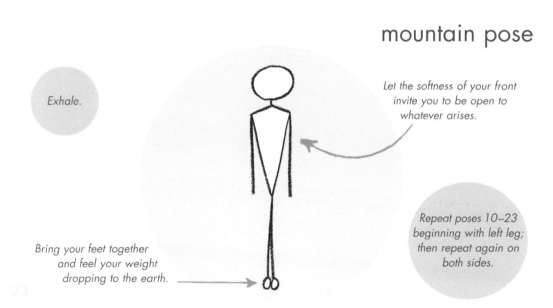

Exhale.

Let the softness of your front invite you to be open to whatever arises.

Repeat poses 10–23 beginning with left leg; then repeat again on both sides.

Bring your feet together and feel your weight dropping to the earth.

23

mountain pose

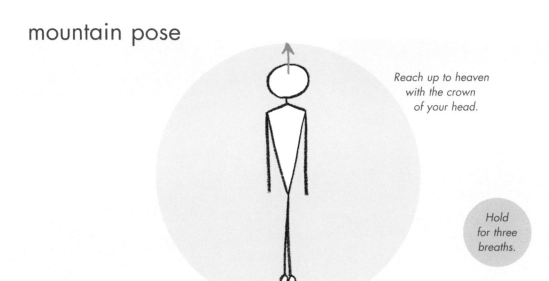

Reach up to heaven
with the crown
of your head.

Hold
for three
breaths.

mountain pose, arms up

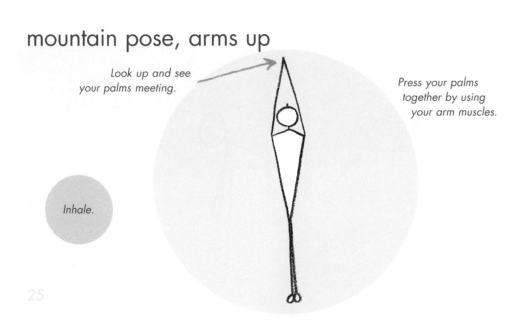

Look up and see
your palms meeting.

Press your palms
together by using
your arm muscles.

Inhale.

standing forward bend

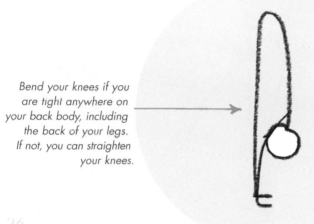

Bend your knees if you are tight anywhere on your back body, including the back of your legs. If not, you can straighten your knees.

Extend your spine in two directions. Go for length rather than trying to touch your nose to your legs.

Exhale.

lunge, right leg back

Spine stays long.

Keep the chest open.

Reach through your back heel so that back leg is long.

Inhale.

downward dog

Press your thighbones into your hamstrings as if they were moving into the seams of "your pantyhose."

Exhale.

Make sure your index fingers and thumbs are pressed flat into the floor.

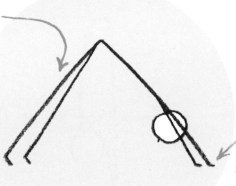

28

plank pose

Slightly tone your belly to support the spine.

Inhale.

Extend energy out through your heels.

Keep arms and legs straight.

Keep wrists below shoulders.

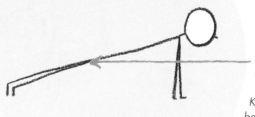

29

knees, chest, chin

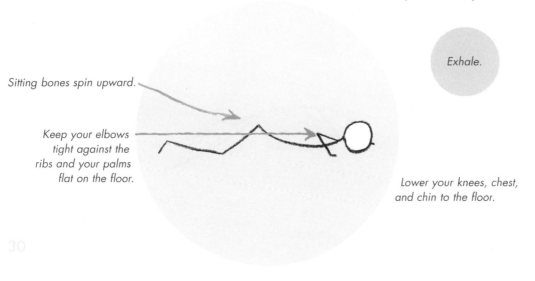

30

Sitting bones spin upward.

Keep your elbows tight against the ribs and your palms flat on the floor.

Exhale.

Lower your knees, chest, and chin to the floor.

baby cobra

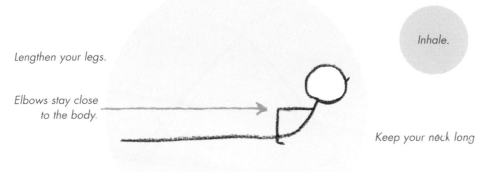

31

Lengthen your legs.

Elbows stay close to the body.

Slide the hips forward to lift the chest.

Inhale.

Keep your neck long

child's pose

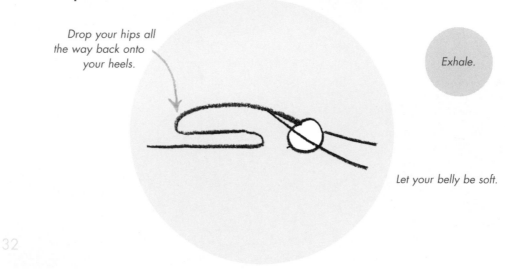

Drop your hips all the way back onto your heels.

Exhale.

Let your belly be soft.

32

downward dog

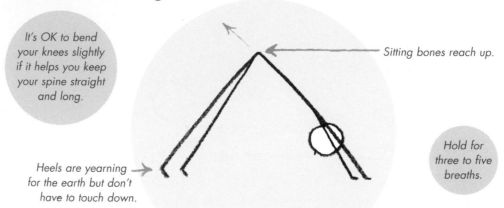

It's OK to bend your knees slightly if it helps you keep your spine straight and long.

Sitting bones reach up.

Heels are yearning for the earth but don't have to touch down.

Hold for three to five breaths.

Your arms push the floor away.

33

lunge, right leg forward

Spine stays long.

Exhale.

Step your right foot all the way up between your hands. You can use your right hand to adjust it forward if you need to.

34

warrior one

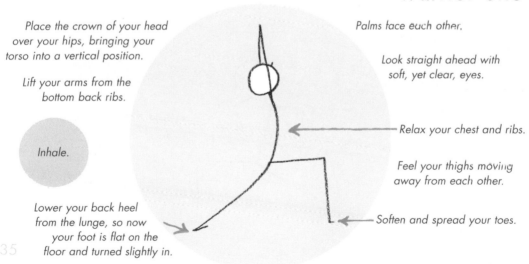

Place the crown of your head over your hips, bringing your torso into a vertical position.

Lift your arms from the bottom back ribs.

Inhale.

Lower your back heel from the lunge, so now your foot is flat on the floor and turned slightly in.

Palms face each other.

Look straight ahead with soft, yet clear, eyes.

Relax your chest and ribs.

Feel your thighs moving away from each other.

Soften and spread your toes.

35

warrior two

Exhale.

Keep your spine vertical.

Reach through your back heel so that back leg is long.

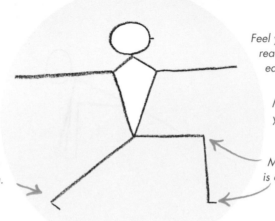

Feel your two middle fingers reaching away from each other.

Make space between your shoulder blades.

Make sure this knee is over this foot.

36

cartwheel

Circle your back arm up and over, then place both hands on the floor on either side of your front foot.

Inhale.

37

lunge, right leg forward

Hold inhale from cartwheel.

Spine stays long.

Reach through your back heel so that back leg is long.

Keep the chest open.

downward dog

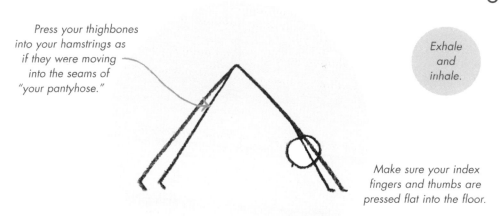

Press your thighbones into your hamstrings as if they were moving into the seams of "your pantyhose."

Exhale and inhale.

Make sure your index fingers and thumbs are pressed flat into the floor.

lunge, left leg forward

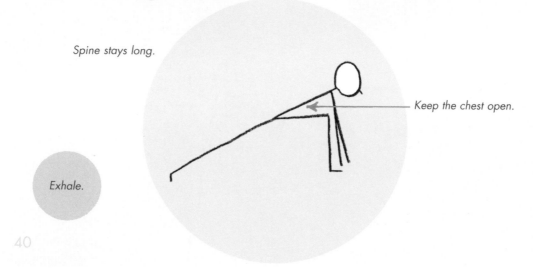

Spine stays long.

Keep the chest open.

Exhale.

40

warrior one

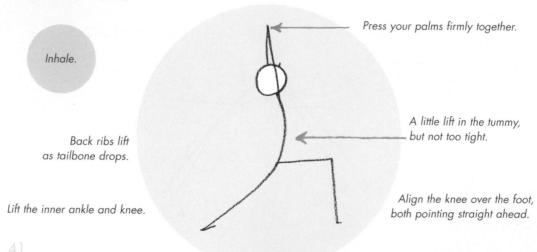

Inhale.

Press your palms firmly together.

Back ribs lift as tailbone drops.

A little lift in the tummy, but not too tight.

Lift the inner ankle and knee.

Align the knee over the foot, both pointing straight ahead.

41

warrior two

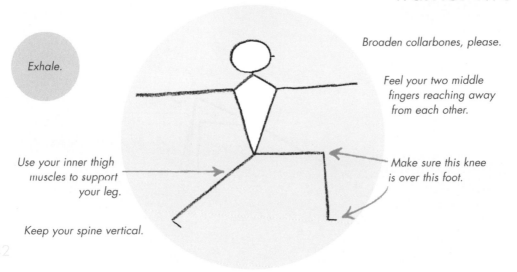

Exhale.

Broaden collarbones, please.

Feel your two middle fingers reaching away from each other.

Use your inner thigh muscles to support your leg.

Make sure this knee is over this foot.

Keep your spine vertical.

cartwheel

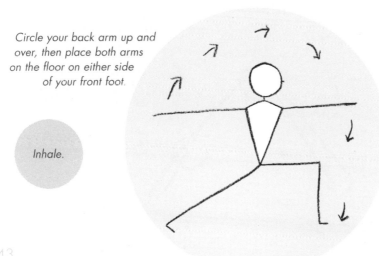

Circle your back arm up and over, then place both arms on the floor on either side of your front foot.

Inhale.

lunge, left leg forward

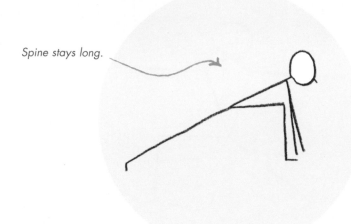

Spine stays long.

Hold inhale from cartwheel.

44

downward dog

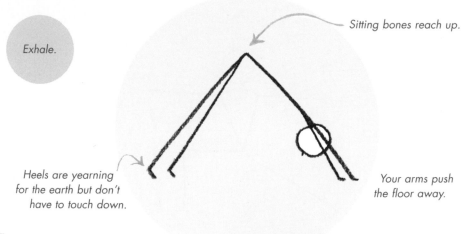

Exhale.

Sitting bones reach up.

Heels are yearning for the earth but don't have to touch down.

Your arms push the floor away.

45

plank pose

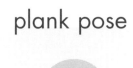

Slightly tone your belly to support the spine.

Inhale.

Extend energy out through your heels.

Keep arms and legs straight.

Keep wrists below shoulders.

46

knees, chest, chin

Sitting bones spin upward.

Lower your knees, chest, and chin to the floor.

Exhale.

Keep your elbows tight against the ribs and your palms flat on the floor.

47

baby cobra

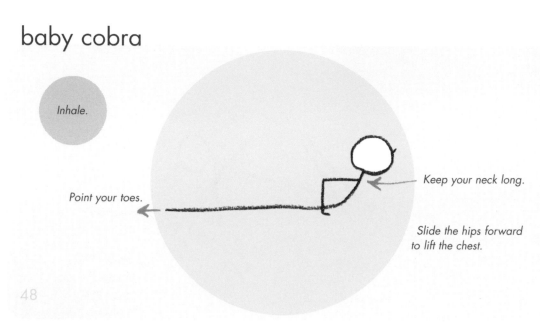

Inhale.

Keep your neck long.

Point your toes.

Slide the hips forward
to lift the chest.

48

child's pose

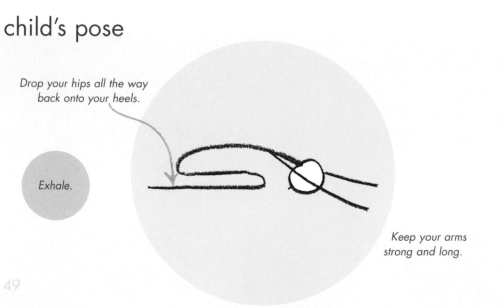

Drop your hips all the way
back onto your heels.

Exhale.

Keep your arms
strong and long.

49

downward dog

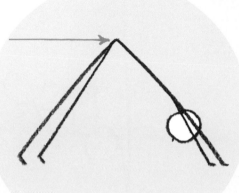

Create length in your spine by reaching pelvis away from hands.

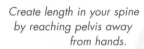

Hold for three to five breaths.

Make sure your index fingers and thumbs are pressed flat into the floor.

50

lunge, right leg forward

Inhale.

Spine stays long.

Keep the chest open.

51

standing forward bend

Do not bounce or try to stretch your legs more. Instead, engage the leg muscles actively, breathe deeply, and cultivate patience.

Exhale.

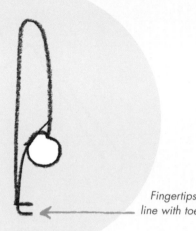

Fingertips are in line with toe tips.

52

powerful pose

Keep your arms by your ears.

Straighten your arms.

Keep your gaze slightly down and forward.

Inhale.

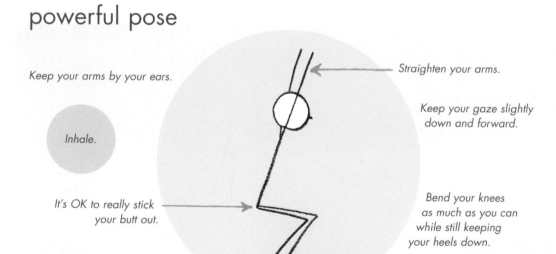

It's OK to really stick your butt out.

Bend your knees as much as you can while still keeping your heels down.

53

mountain pose, arms up

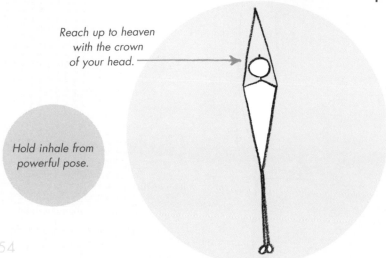

Reach up to heaven with the crown of your head.

Hold inhale from powerful pose.

mountain pose with prayer hands

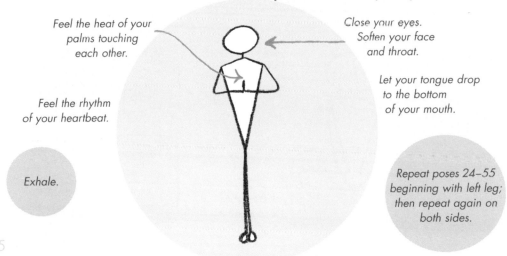

Feel the heat of your palms touching each other.

Close your eyes. Soften your face and throat.

Feel the rhythm of your heartbeat.

Let your tongue drop to the bottom of your mouth.

Exhale.

Repeat poses 24–55 beginning with left leg; then repeat again on both sides.

tree pose

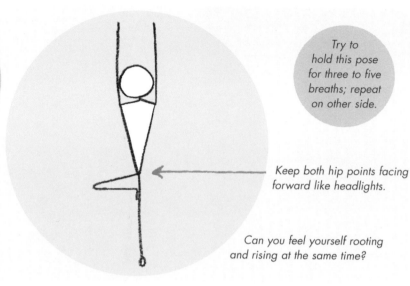

Imagine that you are a tree and that the dirt is at your waist. Your legs are the roots, your spine is the trunk, and your arms are the branches.

Try to hold this pose for three to five breaths; repeat on other side.

Keep both hip points facing forward like headlights.

Can you feel yourself rooting and rising at the same time?

cobbler's pose

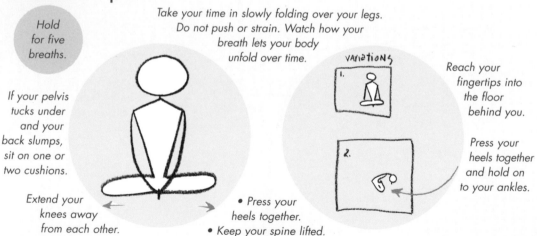

Hold for five breaths.

Take your time in slowly folding over your legs. Do not push or strain. Watch how your breath lets your body unfold over time.

VARIATIONS

1.

2.

Reach your fingertips into the floor behind you.

Press your heels together and hold on to your ankles.

If your pelvis tucks under and your back slumps, sit on one or two cushions.

Extend your knees away from each other.

- Press your heels together.
- Keep your spine lifted.

seated spinal twist

58

Hold for three to five breaths on each side.

You can even take your eyes around the corner.

Push down into the floor to help lift your spine.

Make sure you change legs and twist in both directions.

Rotate your inner organs.

Place this foot flat on the floor, on the outside of the other leg.

half wheel

59

Let your chin fall away from your chest, and soften your throat.

Press down with your arms.

Keep knees right over ankles.

Your feet can be hip distance apart.

Press down with your feet. Raise your hips.

Hold for three to five breaths.

legs up the wall

You can stay in this pose as long as you want.

Keep your legs as close to or far from the wall as feels comfortable—no strain on the back of your legs, please.

Let your sitting bones drop so that you are in a slight back bend.

Relax your torso and chest.

It's nice to place an eye pillow on your eyes.

You can place a rolled towel under your neck, a little pillow under your head, and a folded-up blanket under your back.

60

corpse pose

You can also simply lie down flat on the ground and rest.

Close your eyes. An eye pillow can be nice.

Turn your palms up.

Rest here a minute or as long as you'd like.

Feet should be about hip distance apart.

A pillow under your knees can feel good to your lower back.

61

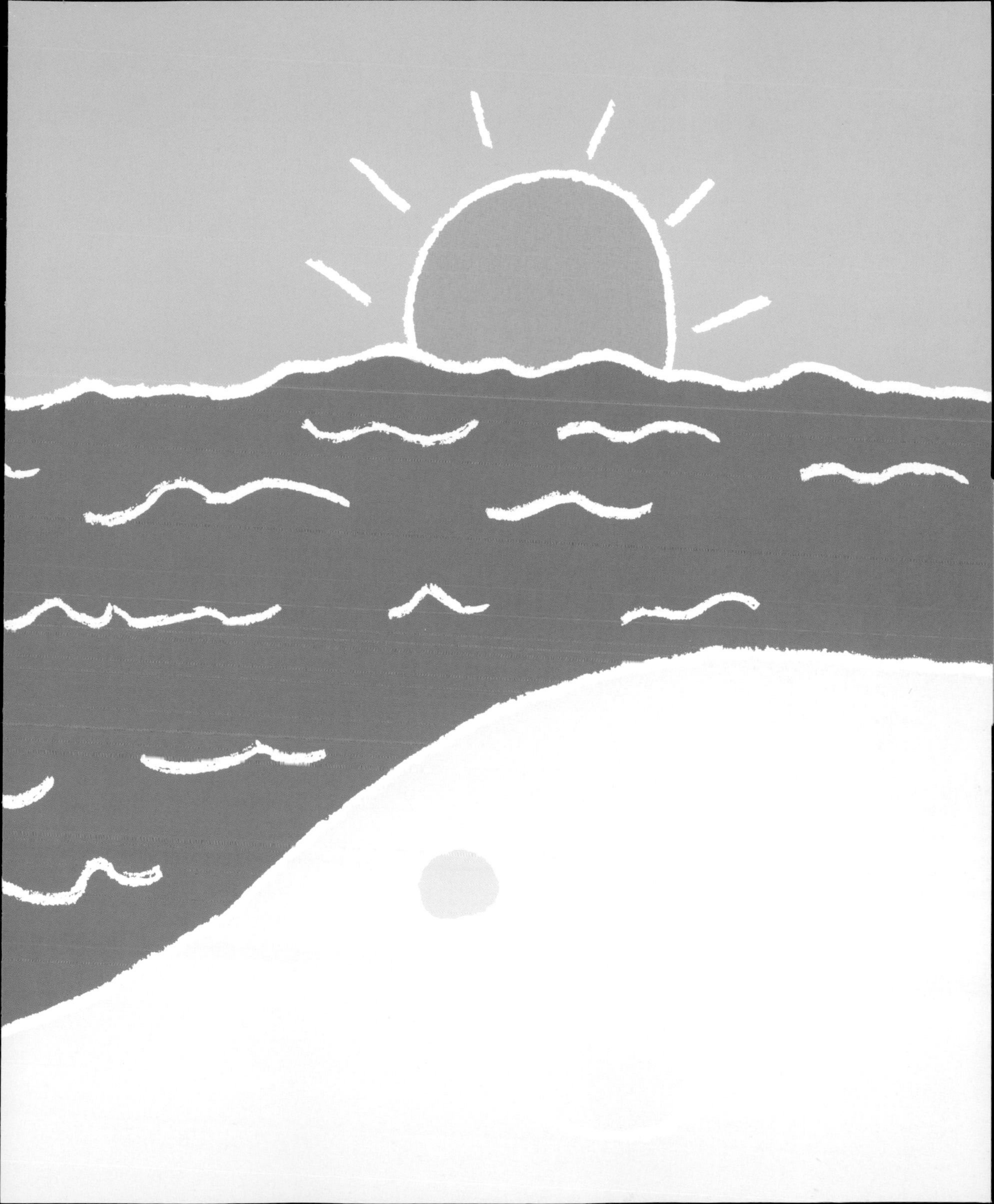

thirty minutes

Thirty-Minute Session

One of my yoga students told me about a Saturday afternoon when she was in a bad mood and acting very grumpy toward her family. Finally her husband begged her, "Go into the bedroom and do some of that yoga stuff!" He didn't really know what yoga was and certainly had no interest in trying it for himself, but he knew that when his wife did her yoga practice, the whole family benefited.

An interesting twist in life is that we cannot truly be of help to others if we don't develop our own inner and outer vitality. Taking care of your body by developing strength, and taking care of your mind by giving yourself space to empty and rest—these are important first steps toward caring for others.

For some of us, the main challenge is reserving time just for ourselves. It's true that sometimes you must put others first—babies can't feed themselves, after all. But after we have dropped off all the kids in the carpool, completed the final negotiations on that pressing business matter, bought the groceries, and picked up the dry cleaning, we are simply too pooped to do yoga.

Making yourself the last priority is not recommended. If you want others around you—your children, husband, boss, coworkers—to feel capable, strong, energized, openhearted, clear-thinking, and confident, you need to cultivate those qualities in yourself. You wouldn't want a piano teacher who couldn't play the piano or a minister who never prayed. Good leaders walked the same path we all have to follow in order to develop any ability: practice! And it takes time.

You may find that when you begin your yoga practice you are constantly running through to-do lists and revisiting past events—all this activity happens inside your head. These thoughts can be so intense and seemingly solid that it is hard to let go of them and simply be present with your immediate experience. This is natural, and for most of us it takes about twenty minutes for this pattern to shift.

This thirty-minute practice includes sun salutations, delicious hip openers and spinal twists, and a simple inversion. Take these thirty minutes as an opportunity to experience the processing effects of yoga and meditation. Your own mind will become clearer while you build muscular, skeletal, and cardiovascular strength. This is how you can begin to develop physical vitality, mental alertness, and a heart that is both soft and strong—all the requirements for truly helping those other people you care about so much.

Thirty-Minute Session

1 sitting meditation: five minutes

2 calming breath with arms: five times

3 cat pose

4 cow pose

5 threading the needle to the right

6 threading the needle to the left (repeat 5 and 6 on other side)

7 downward dog

8 feet walking meditation

9 mountain pose

10 mountain pose, arms up

11 standing forward bend

12 lunge, right leg back

13 downward dog

14 plank pose

15 knees, chest, chin

16 baby cobra

17 child's pose

18 downward dog

19 lunge, right leg forward

20 standing forward bend

21 mountain pose, arms up

22 mountain pose

Repeat poses 10–22 on the left side. Then repeat both sides again.

23 mountain pose

24 mountain pose, arms up

25 standing forward bend

26 lunge, right leg back

27 downward dog

28 plank pose

29 knees, chest, chin

30 baby cobra

31 child's pose

32 downward dog

33 lunge, right leg forward

34 warrior one

35 warrior two

36 cartwheel

37 lunge, right leg forward

38 downward dog

39 lunge, left leg forward

Thirty-Minute Session

40 warrior one

41 warrior two

42 cartwheel

43 lunge, left
leg forward

44 downward dog

45 plank pose

46 knees, chest, chin

47 baby cobra

48 child's pose

49 downward dog

50 lunge, right
leg forward

51 standing forward
bend

52 powerful pose

53 mountain pose,
arms up

54 mountain pose
with prayer hands

Repeat
poses 23–54
with the left leg.
Repeat each
side again.

55 mountain pose

56 mountain pose,
arms up

57 standing forward
bend

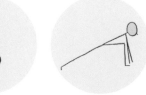

58 lunge, right
leg back

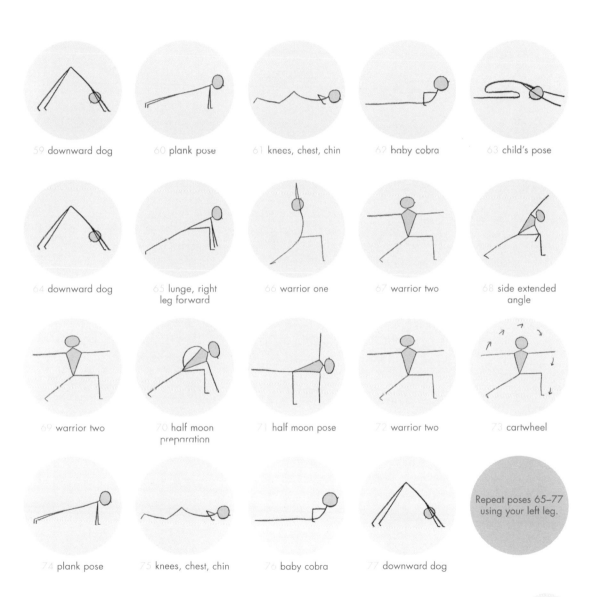

59 downward dog

60 plank pose

61 knees, chest, chin

62 baby cobra

63 child's pose

64 downward dog

65 lunge, right leg forward

66 warrior one

67 warrior two

68 side extended angle

69 warrior two

70 half moon preparation

71 half moon pose

72 warrior two

73 cartwheel

74 plank pose

75 knees, chest, chin

76 baby cobra

77 downward dog

Repeat poses 65–77 using your left leg.

Thirty-Minute Session

78 jumping in
downward dog

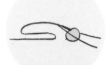

79 child's pose

80 downward dog

81 downward dog
split

82 pigeon pose

Repeat poses 81–82
using your left leg.

83 downward dog

84 plank and lie
down on tummy

85 locust pose, lifting
upper body

86 locust pose,
lifting legs

87 locust pose

Repeat poses 84–87
three times.

88 bow pose

89 supine spinal twist
(repeat on other side)

90 star pose

91 shoulder stand
preparation

92 shoulder stand,
hips up

93 shoulder stand,
legs off wall

94 corpse pose

sitting meditation: three minutes

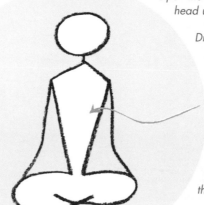

You might not find it easy to sit like this at first, but as you begin to rest your mind, you may begin to experience a sense of ease.

Open the crown of your head up to heaven.

Drop your tongue.

Soften your throat.

Feel your rib cage expand and contract as you breathe.

Relax your face and your judgment.

Rest your palms on your thighs. This is called the mudra of calm abiding.

Cross your legs in a way that is comfortable for you. Try sitting on a cushion.

Let your sitting bones drop down into the earth.

calming breath with arms: five times

Inhale evenly, drawing your breath down as your arms float all the way up next to your ears.

Exhale smoothly, keeping the spine lifted as the arms lower down to the floor.

cat pose

Exhale.

Tuck your tailbone and head under.

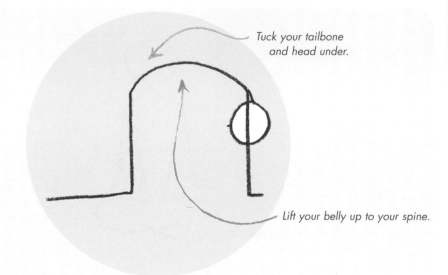

Lift your belly up to your spine.

3

cow pose

Keep enough length in the back of your neck that someone could kiss you there.

Lift your chest and face up.

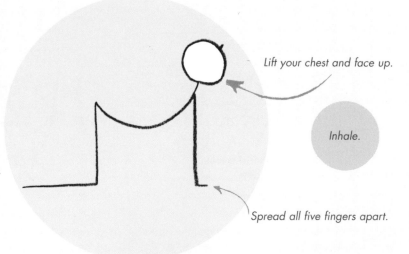

Inhale.

Stretch your sitting bones to the sky.

Spread all five fingers apart.

4

threading the needle to the right

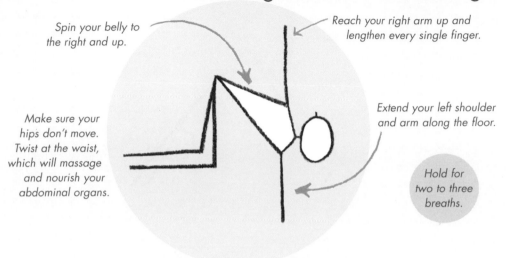

Spin your belly to the right and up.

Reach your right arm up and lengthen every single finger.

Make sure your hips don't move. Twist at the waist, which will massage and nourish your abdominal organs.

Extend your left shoulder and arm along the floor.

Hold for two to three breaths.

threading the needle to the left

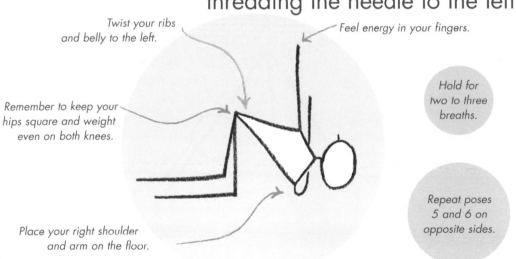

Twist your ribs and belly to the left.

Feel energy in your fingers.

Remember to keep your hips square and weight even on both knees.

Hold for two to three breaths.

Place your right shoulder and arm on the floor.

Repeat poses 5 and 6 on opposite sides.

downward dog

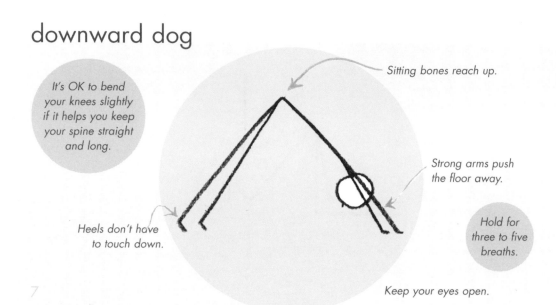

It's OK to bend your knees slightly if it helps you keep your spine straight and long.

Sitting bones reach up.

Strong arms push the floor away.

Heels don't have to touch down.

Hold for three to five breaths.

7

Keep your eyes open.

feet walking meditation

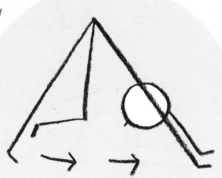

Slowly walk your feet to your hands as if you were doing a walking meditation. Feel the texture of the floor as you move toe, ball, heel.

Bend your knees whenever you need to.

8*

*For poses 9–54, see pages 31–53

mountain pose

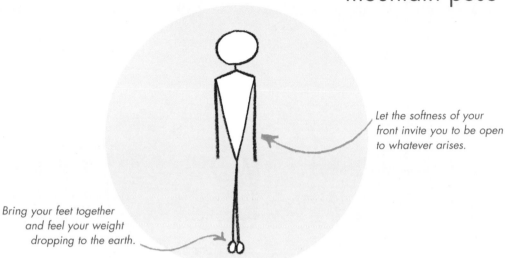

Let the softness of your front invite you to be open to whatever arises.

Bring your feet together and feel your weight dropping to the earth.

55

mountain pose, arms up

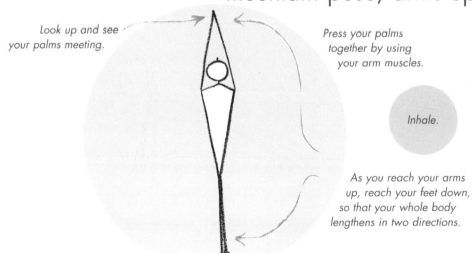

Look up and see your palms meeting.

Press your palms together by using your arm muscles.

Inhale.

As you reach your arms up, reach your feet down, so that your whole body lengthens in two directions.

56

standing forward bend

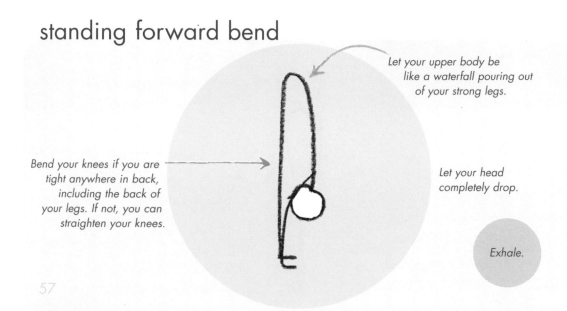

Let your upper body be like a waterfall pouring out of your strong legs.

Bend your knees if you are tight anywhere in back, including the back of your legs. If not, you can straighten your knees.

Let your head completely drop.

Exhale.

57

lunge, right leg back

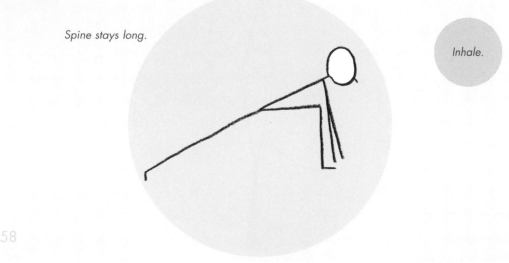

Spine stays long.

Inhale.

58

downward dog

Hold this downward-facing dog for three to five breaths. A breath means one complete inhale and exhale.

Create length in your spine by reaching pelvis away from hands.

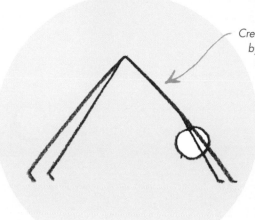

Exhale.

59

plank pose

Inhale.

Extend energy out through your heels.

Keep arms and legs straight.

Slightly tone your belly to support the spine.

Keep wrists below your shoulders.

60

knees, chest, chin

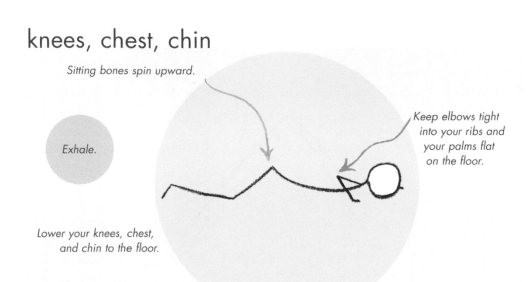

Sitting bones spin upward.

Exhale.

Keep elbows tight
into your ribs and
your palms flat
on the floor.

Lower your knees, chest,
and chin to the floor.

61

baby cobra

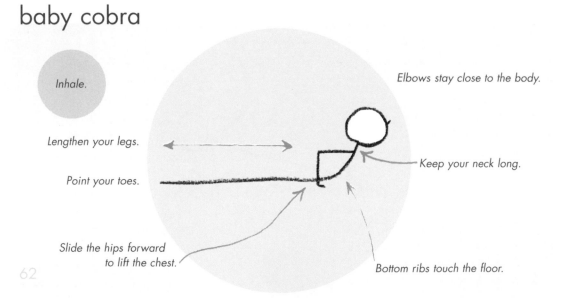

Inhale.

Elbows stay close to the body.

Lengthen your legs.

Point your toes.

Keep your neck long.

Slide the hips forward
to lift the chest.

Bottom ribs touch the floor.

62

child's pose

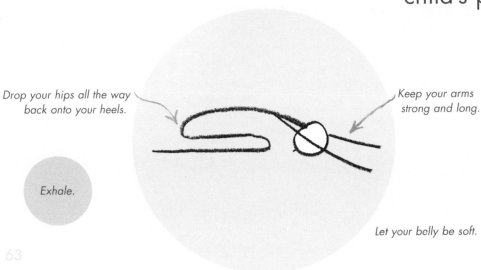

Drop your hips all the way back onto your heels.

Keep your arms strong and long.

Exhale.

63

Let your belly be soft.

downward dog

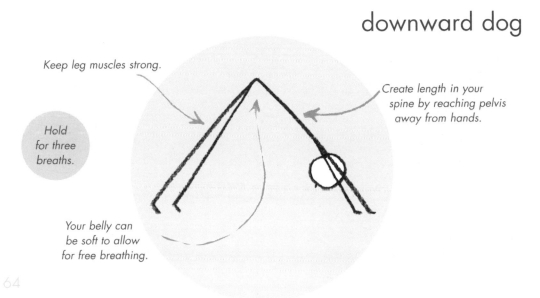

Keep leg muscles strong.

Create length in your spine by reaching pelvis away from hands.

Hold for three breaths.

Your belly can be soft to allow for free breathing.

64

lunge, right leg forward

Exhale.

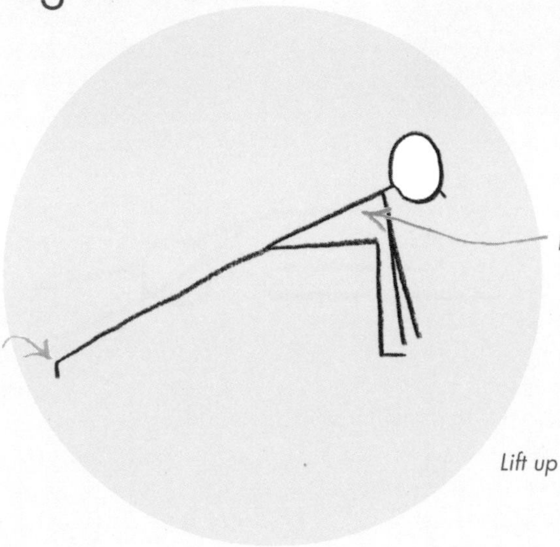

Spine stays long.

Reach through your back heel so that back leg is long.

Keep the chest open.

Lift up onto your fingertips.

65

warrior one

Inhale.

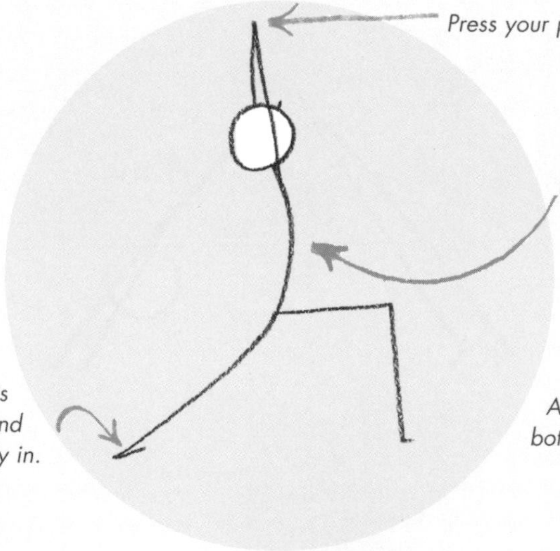

Press your palms firmly together.

A little lift in the tummy, but not too tight.

Back ribs lift as tailbone drops.

Your back foot is flat on the floor and turned slightly in.

Align the knee over the foot, both pointing straight ahead.

66

warrior two

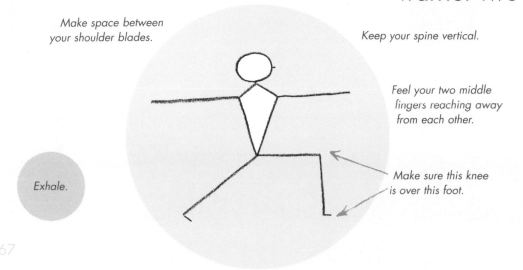

Make space between your shoulder blades.

Keep your spine vertical.

Feel your two middle fingers reaching away from each other.

Exhale.

Make sure this knee is over this foot.

side extended angle

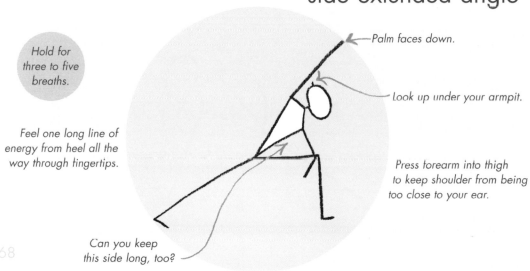

Hold for three to five breaths.

Palm faces down.

Look up under your armpit.

Feel one long line of energy from heel all the way through fingertips.

Press forearm into thigh to keep shoulder from being too close to your ear.

Can you keep this side long, too?

warrior two

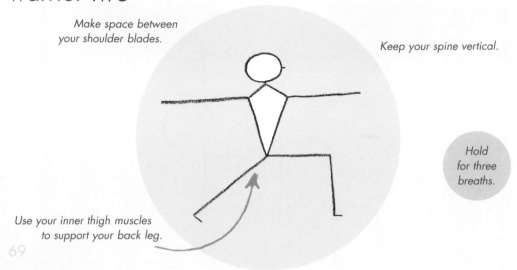

Make space between your shoulder blades.

Keep your spine vertical.

Hold for three breaths.

Use your inner thigh muscles to support your back leg.

69

half moon preparation

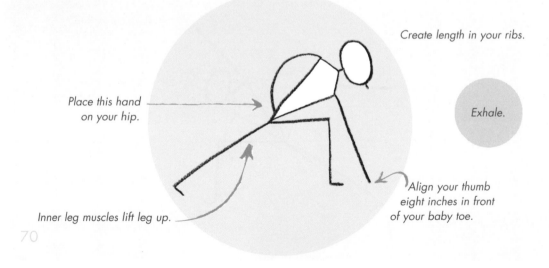

Create length in your ribs.

Place this hand on your hip.

Exhale.

Align your thumb eight inches in front of your baby toe.

Inner leg muscles lift leg up.

70

half moon pose

You can look up, down, or forward.

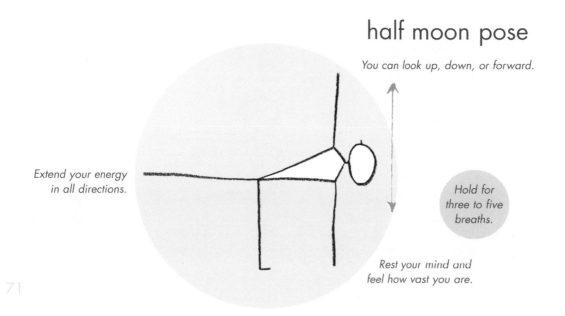

Extend your energy in all directions.

Hold for three to five breaths.

Rest your mind and feel how vast you are.

warrior two

Keep your spine vertical.

Make space between your shoulder blades.

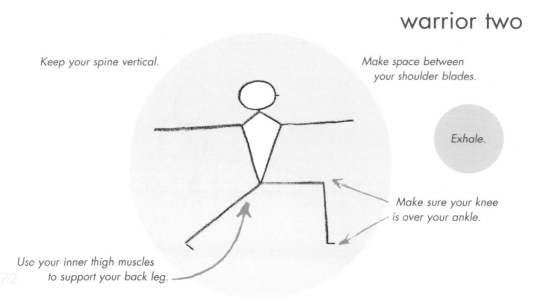

Exhale.

Make sure your knee is over your ankle.

Use your inner thigh muscles to support your back leg.

cartwheel

Circle your back arm up and over, then place both arms on the floor on either side of your front foot.

Inhale.

plank pose

Hold inhale from cartwheel.

Keep arms and legs straight.

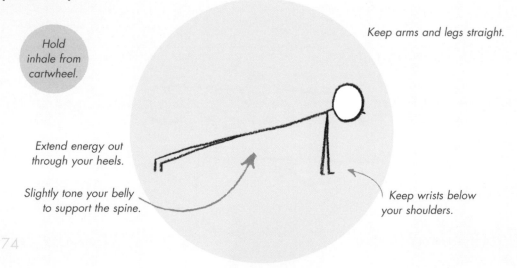

Extend energy out through your heels.

Slightly tone your belly to support the spine.

Keep wrists below your shoulders.

knees, chest, chin

Sitting bones spin upward.

Keep elbows tight into your ribs and your palms flat on the floor.

Exhale.

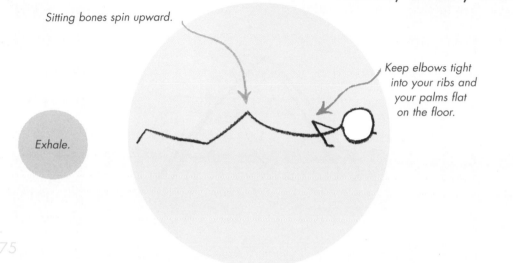

baby cobra

Inhale.

Lengthen your legs.

Point your toes.

Elbows stay close to the body.

Slide the hips forward to lift the chest.

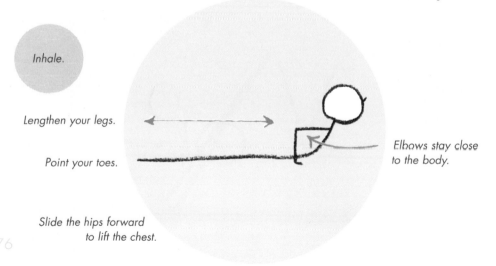

downward dog

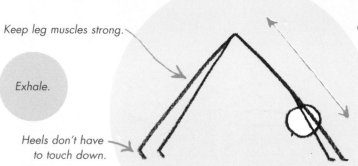

Keep leg muscles strong.

Create length in your spine by reaching pelvis away from hands.

Exhale.

Heels don't have to touch down.

Repeat poses 65–76 using your left leg.

77

jumping in downward dog

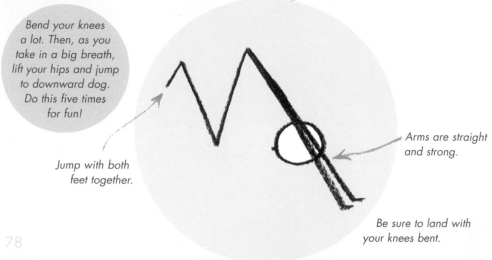

Bend your knees a lot. Then, as you take in a big breath, lift your hips and jump to downward dog. Do this five times for fun!

Jump with both feet together.

Arms are straight and strong.

Be sure to land with your knees bent.

78

child's pose

Drop your hips all the way back onto your heels.

Keep your arms strong and long.

Hold for three to five breaths.

Let your belly be soft.

downward dog

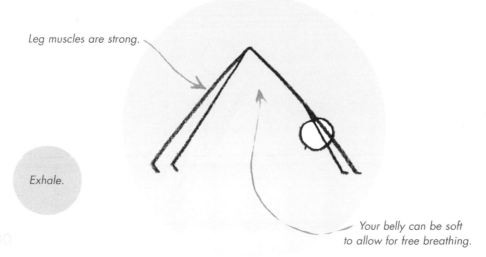

Leg muscles are strong.

Exhale.

Your belly can be soft to allow for free breathing.

downward dog split

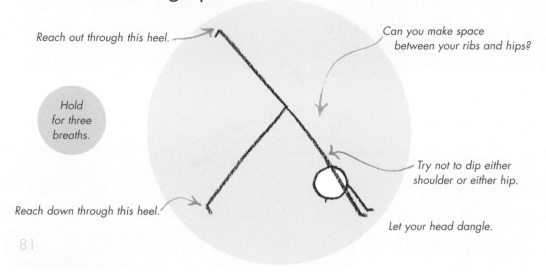

Reach out through this heel.

Can you make space between your ribs and hips?

Hold for three breaths.

Try not to dip either shoulder or either hip.

Reach down through this heel.

Let your head dangle.

81

pigeon pose

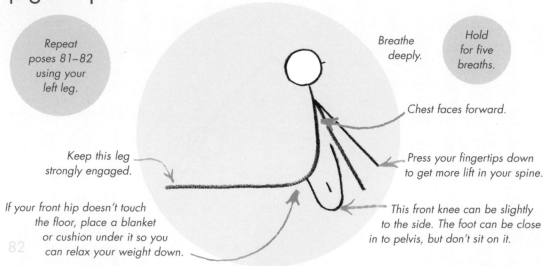

Repeat poses 81–82 using your left leg.

Breathe deeply.

Hold for five breaths.

Chest faces forward.

Keep this leg strongly engaged.

Press your fingertips down to get more lift in your spine.

If your front hip doesn't touch the floor, place a blanket or cushion under it so you can relax your weight down.

This front knee can be slightly to the side. The foot can be close in to pelvis, but don't sit on it.

82

downward dog

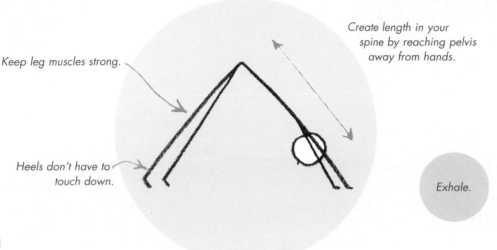

Keep leg muscles strong.

Create length in your spine by reaching pelvis away from hands.

Heels don't have to touch down.

Exhale.

plank and lie down on tummy

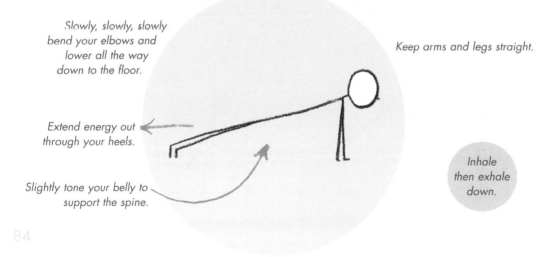

Slowly, slowly, slowly bend your elbows and lower all the way down to the floor.

Keep arms and legs straight.

Extend energy out through your heels.

Slightly tone your belly to support the spine.

Inhale then exhale down.

locust pose, lifting upper body

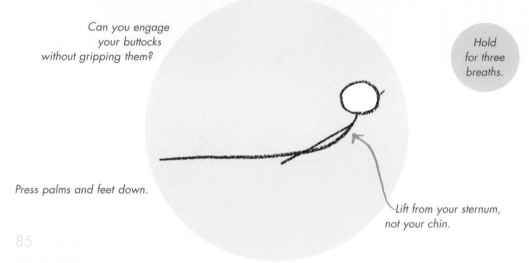

Can you engage your buttocks without gripping them?

Hold for three breaths.

Press palms and feet down.

Lift from your sternum, not your chin.

85

locust pose, lifting legs

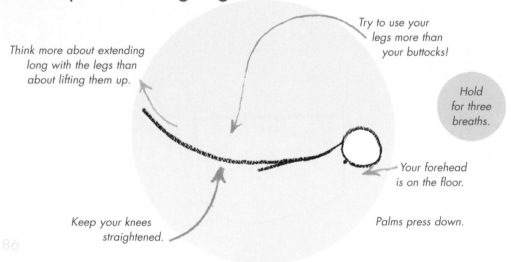

Try to use your legs more than your buttocks!

Think more about extending long with the legs than about lifting them up.

Hold for three breaths.

Your forehead is on the floor.

Keep your knees straightened.

Palms press down.

86

locust pose

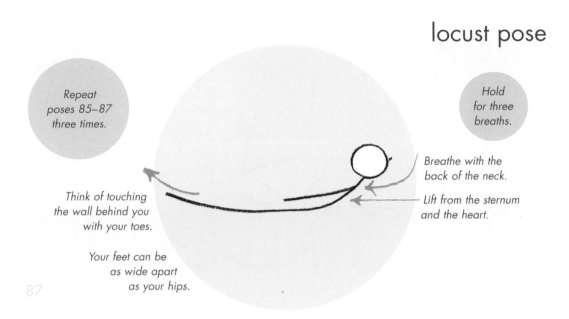

Repeat poses 85–87 three times.

Hold for three breaths.

Breathe with the back of the neck.

Think of touching the wall behind you with your toes.

Lift from the sternum and the heart.

Your feet can be as wide apart as your hips.

87

bow pose

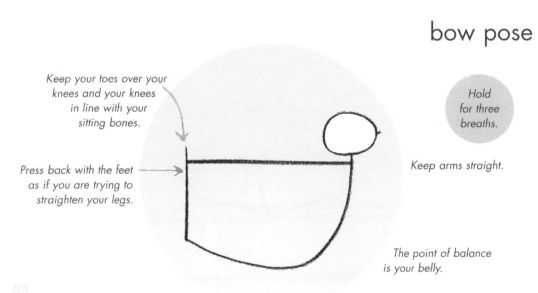

Keep your toes over your knees and your knees in line with your sitting bones.

Hold for three breaths.

Press back with the feet as if you are trying to straighten your legs.

Keep arms straight.

The point of balance is your belly.

88

supine spinal twist

Relax your neck
and throat.

It's OK if you can't stack
the top knee directly over
the bottom one.

Release your weight
into the floor.

Repeat on
other side; hold
for three to five
breaths on
each side.

Turn the palms up.

89

star pose

Fold over softly and
rest your head in the
lap of your feet.
If it doesn't reach,
put a pillow
on your feet.

Don't tug with your
arms. Just relax....

Hold for
five to eight
breaths.

Your feet can be
about two feet away
from your hips.

90

shoulder stand preparation

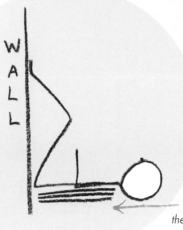

When you get organized into this set-up, press your elbows down at the same time that you push your feet into the wall, and your hips will go right up.

Your neck and head should not be touching the blankets.

Fold up three firm blankets and place them under your back.

shoulder stand, hips up

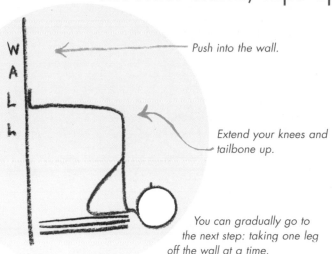

You can stay here for five to ten breaths.

Push into the wall.

Extend your knees and tailbone up.

You can gradually go to the next step: taking one leg off the wall at a time.

shoulder stand, legs off wall

You can stay here for five to ten breaths. Over time you can work up to five minutes.

With Barbie doll feet, reach through the tips of your toes and relax your ankles.

Zip your inner thighs together.

Look up at your toes.

Try to relax your throat and let your chin and forehead fall away from your chest.

Rewind to come out of shoulder stand: feet on the wall, slowly lower hips, rest for three to five breaths, roll over to one side and slowly sit up.

93

corpse pose

You can also simply lie down flat on the ground and rest.

Stay here as long as you like.

Close your eyes. An eye pillow can be nice.

Feet should be about hip distance apart.

A pillow under your knees can feel good to your lower back.

Turn your palms up.

94

Sixty-Minute Session

An hour! Ahh, finally a real, significant chunk of time—open, empty, just waiting for me. Then why am I not jumping at this opportunity? Why is it that at the very last minute I feel like I have a headache, or am just so tired, or really want to go shopping or eat chocolate?

These are the same questions I asked myself the summer I was invited to participate in the resident hermit program at Omega Institute. They were providing me with ten days of time, space, housing, and meals. No cooking, no cleaning, no teaching, no talking. All I had to do was practice yoga, meditate, and write. Heaven!

After getting settled into the luxury cabin in the woods, I sat on the deck and looked at the sky. Then I took a nap. Then it was time for dinner. Then I called my husband on my cell phone just to say good night. I went to bed. I was surprised to find that I woke up naturally to the sound of the birds singing at 6 A.M. Beautiful! Peaceful! I made coffee and lay in bed with a book for as long as I felt like it. I got up and took a leisurely shower. Then I looked at the clock. It was 9 A.M. Suddenly the day seemed way too long and quiet and empty.

For the first two days after getting settled I did various cleaning rituals—washing the dishes, organizing my drawing materials, cleaning up my computer desktop—anything that was easy and a good way to avoid actually settling down to work. This is called resistance. It is the common response to doing anything that's good for you, even if it's something you really want to do. Not everybody has this problem, but many of us do, and it seems that the answer is discipline. But if discipline is a challenge for you, trying to be disciplined will only create more resistance.

Here are some tips for working with resistance. First of all, acknowledge it. Yoga is an invitation to meet your own mind as well really feel the tightness in your hamstrings, the thickness in your waist, or the weakness in your arms. It's only natural that this can seem as scary and overwhelming as ten days alone in the woods. But sometimes we don't recognize this because it shows up in other forms.

What does your resistance feel like today? Is it manifesting as crabbiness, a craving for pretzels, a sudden urge to make a phone call, a desire to organize your desk? Is it sluggish or jumpy? Don't try to change the texture of your energy, but do your practice anyway. Try to shift your discipline more toward commitment. Instead of being "good," can you be curious?

Yoga is an unfolding process that is always different and never finished. You don't have to feel enthusiastic and openhearted to do yoga. You can just be you. Rather than locking on to any fixed ideas of how blissful yoga should be or how eager we should feel, recognize that yoga invites us to accept all the parts of ourselves—sweet, harsh, fearful, joyous. However you are feeling, just do the yoga anyway. Let the flavor of your experience be of interest to you and then watch how it shifts as you begin to twist, bend, and deepen your breathing.

In this sixty-minute session, you'll build on the previous sessions and add a calming breath exercise and more challenging inversions.

Sixty-Minute Session

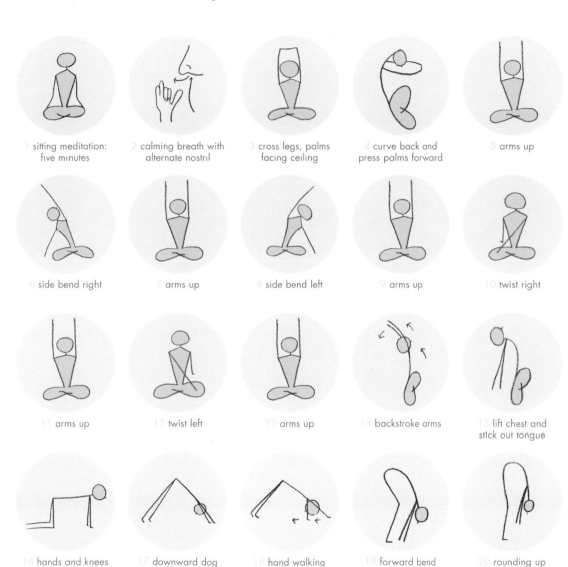

1 sitting meditation: five minutes

2 calming breath with alternate nostril

3 cross legs, palms facing ceiling

4 curve back and press palms forward

5 arms up

6 side bend right

7 arms up

8 side bend left

9 arms up

10 twist right

11 arms up

12 twist left

13 arms up

14 backstroke arms

15 lift chest and stick out tongue

16 hands and knees

17 downward dog

18 hand walking meditation

19 forward bend

20 rounding up

Sixty-Minute Session

21 walking meditation to front of mat

22 mountain pose

23 mountain pose, arms up

24 standing forward bend

25 lunge, right leg back

26 downward dog

27 plank pose

28 knees, chest, chin

29 baby cobra

30 child's pose

31 downward dog

32 lunge, right leg forward

33 standing forward bend

34 mountain pose, arms up

35 mountain pose

Repeat poses 22–35 two times each side.

36 mountain pose

37 mountain pose, arms up

38 standing forward bend

39 lunge, right leg back

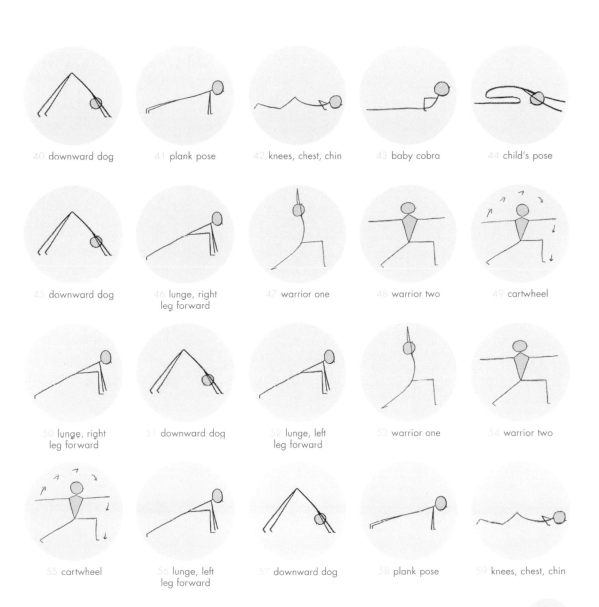

40 downward dog

41 plank pose

42 knees, chest, chin

43 baby cobra

44 child's pose

45 downward dog

46 lunge, right
leg forward

47 warrior one

48 warrior two

49 cartwheel

50 lunge, right
leg forward

51 downward dog

52 lunge, left
leg forward

53 warrior one

54 warrior two

55 cartwheel

56 lunge, left
leg forward

57 downward dog

58 plank pose

59 knees, chest, chin

Sixty-Minute Session

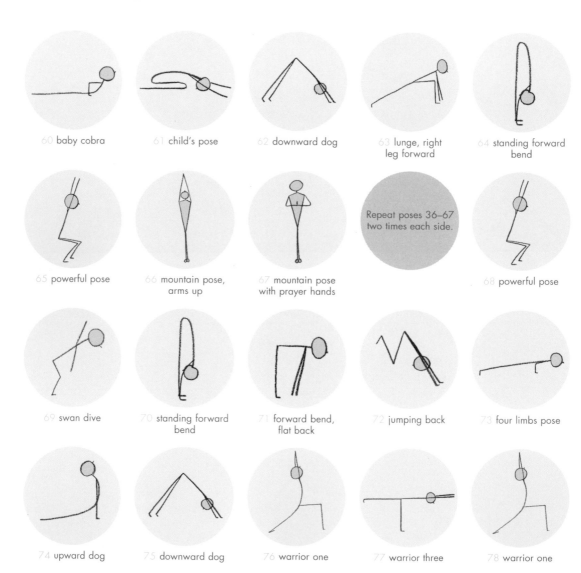

60 baby cobra

61 child's pose

62 downward dog

63 lunge, right leg forward

64 standing forward bend

65 powerful pose

66 mountain pose, arms up

67 mountain pose with prayer hands

Repeat poses 36–67 two times each side.

68 powerful pose

69 swan dive

70 standing forward bend

71 forward bend, flat back

72 jumping back

73 four limbs pose

74 upward dog

75 downward dog

76 warrior one

77 warrior three

78 warrior one

79 warrior two

80 extended side angle

81 triangle pose

82 warrior two

83 cartwheel

84 plank pose

85 four limbs pose

86 upward dog

87 downward dog

88 jumping forward from downward dog

89 forward bend, flat back

90 standing forward bend

91 reverse swan dive

92 powerful pose

93 mountain pose

Repeat poses 68–93 on other side.

94 tree pose (repeat on other side)

95 tree pose with side bend

96 forearm stand preparation

97 forearm stand

Sixty-Minute Session

98 headstand preparation

99 headstand, knees bent at wall

100 headstand

101 child's pose

102 locust pose

103 bow pose

104 half wheel

105 wheel

106 windshield wipers

107 right leg up lying on back, then left

108 straight leg supine twist

109 cobbler's pose

110 head to knee pose (repeat on other side)

111 seated forward bend

112 shoulder stand

113 plow pose

114 corpse pose

sitting meditation: five minutes

You might not find it easy to sit like this at first, but as you begin to rest your mind, you may begin to experience a sense of ease.

Open the crown of your head up to heaven.

Soften your throat.

Feel your rib cage expand and contract as you breathe.

Cross your legs in a way that is comfortable for you. Try sitting on a cushion.

Let your sitting bones drop down into the earth.

1

calming breath with alternate nostril

Breathe in and out through the nose only.

Use your right hand to do this.

Inhale right for six counts and close the right nostril. Exhale left. Continue.

First, place the ring finger on your left nostril and thumb on your right nostril. Exhale completely.

Next, close off your right nostril and inhale left for six counts. Close the left nostril, lift your thumb, and exhale out your right nostril for six counts.

2

cross legs, palms facing ceiling

Palms face the ceiling.

Try to lengthen your inner elbows.

Lengthen up from the sides of the rib cage.

Inhale.

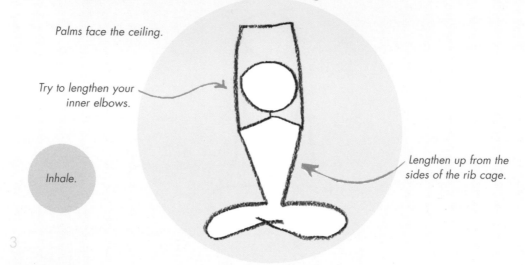

3

curve back and press palms forward

Drop your head.

Can you send your breath into the space between your shoulder blades?

Send your belly button to your spine.

Tuck your pelvis.

Exhale.

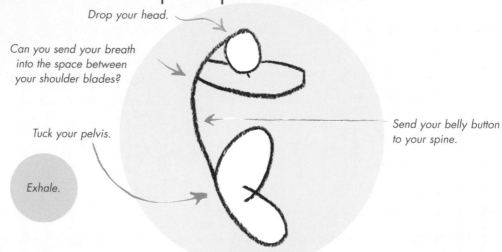

4

arms up

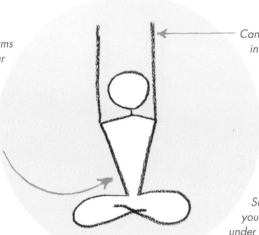

Imagine that your arms begin at the bottom of your back ribs, and lift them from there without scrunching up your shoulders by your ears.

Can you find space in your wrists?

Inhale.

Sit on a cushion if your pelvis is tucking under your lotus legs.

5

side bend right

Your spine curves, but your arm is straight and long.

Exhale.

6

arms up

Inhale.

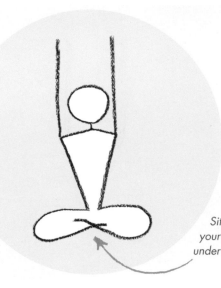

*Sit on a cushion if
your pelvis is tucking
under your lotus legs.*

7

side bend left

Exhale.

*How nice the breath feels
in this expanded rib area.*

*Try not to slump
in this shoulder.*

*Keep both sitting bones
equally grounded.*

8

arms up

Inhale.

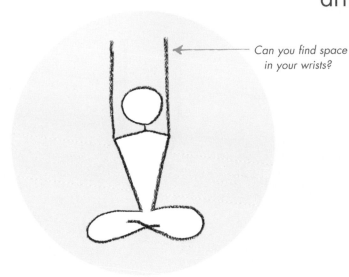

Can you find space
in your wrists?

9

twist right

Relax your neck.

Exhale.

Invite your back muscles
to feel soft and broad.

Make sure this
armpit/chest area
is open.

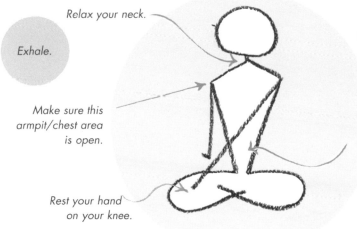

Scoop your belly
around to the right.

Rest your hand
on your knee.

10

arms up

Imagine that your arms begin at the bottom of your back ribs, and lift them from there without scrunching up your shoulders by your ears.

Inhale.

11

twist left

Don't forget to include your head in this twist.

Exhale.

Reach down to the floor with this hand.

Place your right hand on your left thigh; please do not push down on your knee.

12

arms up

Inhale.

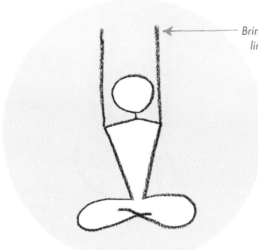

Bring your arms in
line with your ears.

13

backstroke arms

Backstroke your arms as
if you are swimming.

Keep shoulders down.

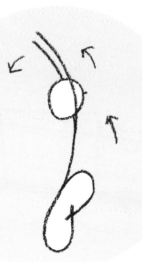

Soften your throat.

Hold the
inhale from
arms up.

14

lift chest and stick out tongue

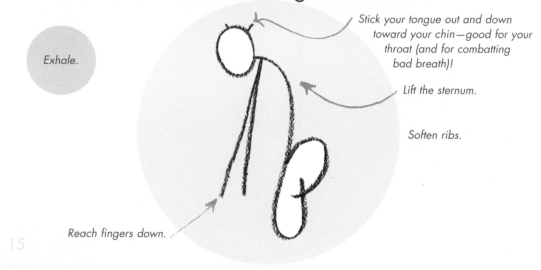

Exhale.

Stick your tongue out and down toward your chin—good for your throat (and for combatting bad breath)!

Lift the sternum.

Soften ribs.

Reach fingers down.

15

hands and knees

Find the length in your spine, from the tailbone to the crown of your head.

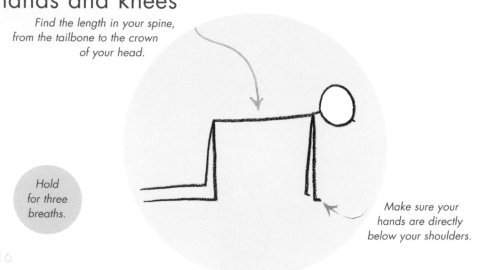

Hold for three breaths.

Make sure your hands are directly below your shoulders.

16

downward dog

Keep leg muscles strong.

Create length in your spine by reaching pelvis away from hands.

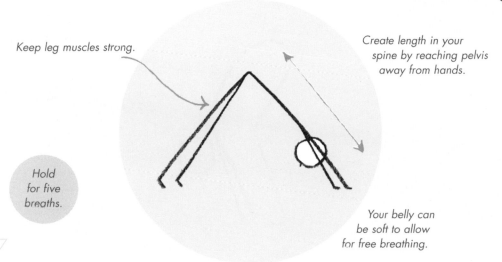

Hold for five breaths.

Your belly can be soft to allow for free breathing.

17

hand walking meditation

How sensitive can you be? Notice the gradual shifting of weight from four things to two things, the texture of your mat under your hands, the subtle changes in your breath. See everything along the way.

Starting from downward dog, slowly walk your hands back to your feet. It's OK to bend your knees at any time.

18

forward bend

Hold for five breaths.

If your hamstrings feel tight, bend your legs.

Let your upper body be like a waterfall.

Let your head completely drop.

19

rounding up

Stack your hips over heels, head over hips.

Slowly round up. Try to feel and visualize every single vertabra.

Let the head dangle, and as you round up, let it be the last thing to come up.

Feet solidly press down.

20

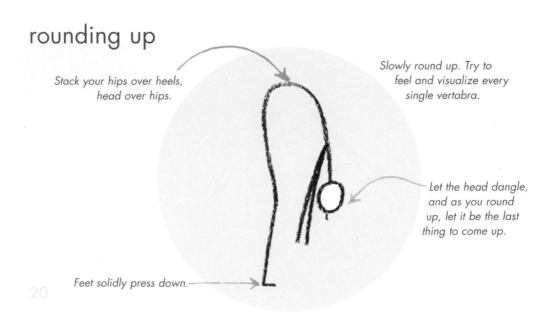

walking meditation to front of mat

In sitting meditation, we use breath as a reference point for returning to and resting in the present moment, but in walking meditation, we use our footsteps.

Rest your gaze at eye level as you are walking, but have an awareness of your environment as well.

21

Feel your feet connecting to the earth.

powerful pose

Straighten your arms.

Keep your arms by your ears.

Keep your gaze slightly down and forward.

Inhale.

Bend your knees as much as you can while still keeping your heels down.

It's OK to really stick your butt out.

68

*For poses 22–67, see pages 31–53

swan dive

Long spine.

Exhale.

Feel the wind you make
as you fold forward.
Touch your hands to
the floor.

You can do this with straight
legs as long as you can
bend at the top of your legs
and not at the waist.

69

standing forward bend

Do not bounce or
try to stretch your legs
more. Instead, engage
the leg muscles actively,
breathe deeply, and
cultivate patience.

Hold the
exhale from the
swan dive.

Bend your knees if you are
tight anywhere on your
back body, including the
back of your legs. If not, you
can straighten your knees.

Keep fingertips in line
with toe tips.

70

forward bend, flat back

Reach your pubic bone and sternum away from each other.

Look forward.

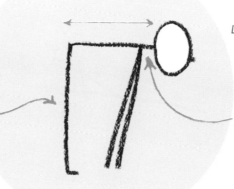

If you feel tight in your hamstrings or lower back, or you can't reach the floor, then it's recommended to bend your knees for this pose.

Feel how the neck is an extension of your spine.

Inhale.

71

jumping back

Exhale.

Jump into downward-facing dog, move into plank, bend elbows into four limbs pose.

72

four limbs pose

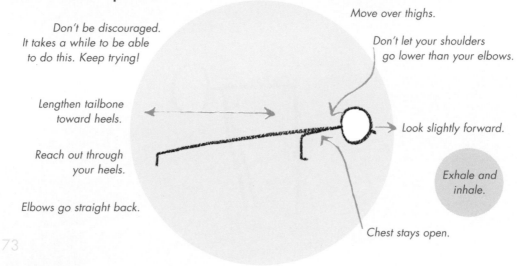

Don't be discouraged. It takes a while to be able to do this. Keep trying!

Lengthen tailbone toward heels.

Reach out through your heels.

Elbows go straight back.

Move over thighs.

Don't let your shoulders go lower than your elbows.

Look slightly forward.

Exhale and inhale.

Chest stays open.

73

upward dog

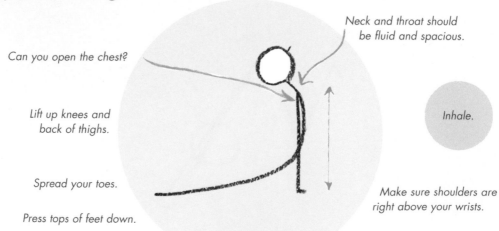

Can you open the chest?

Lift up knees and back of thighs.

Spread your toes.

Press tops of feet down.

Neck and throat should be fluid and spacious.

Inhale.

Make sure shoulders are right above your wrists.

74

downward dog

Sitting bones reach up.

Your arms push the floor away.

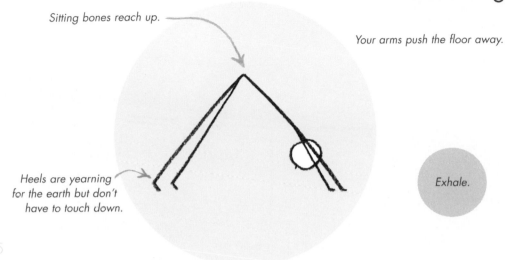

Heels are yearning
for the earth but don't
have to touch down.

Exhale.

75

warrior one

Place the crown of your head
over your hips, bringing your
torso into a vertical position.

Palms face each other.

Look with soft,
yet clear, eyes.

Lift your arms from
the bottom back ribs.

Relax your chest and ribs.

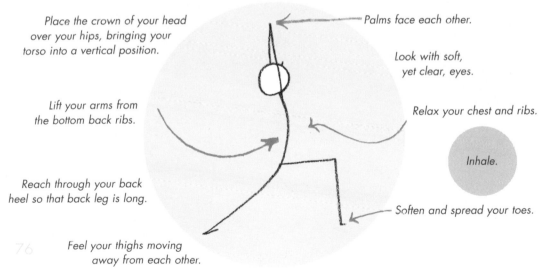

Inhale.

Reach through your back
heel so that back leg is long.

Soften and spread your toes.

76

Feel your thighs moving
away from each other.

warrior three

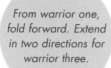

From warrior one, fold forward. Extend in two directions for warrior three.

Keep the back of your neck long by looking down.

Reach out through every finger.

Lift belly up to support your spine.

Try to hold this pose for three to five breaths. Remember: a breath means one complete inhale and exhale.

Flex your foot and strongly reach back so your foot and whole leg feel like someone is pulling your sock off.

77

warrior one

Hold for three to five breaths.

Press your palms firmly together.

A little lift in the tummy, but not too tight.

Back ribs lift as tailbone drops.

Align the knee over the foot, both pointing straight ahead.

78   Lift the inner ankle and knee.

warrior two

Keep your spine vertical.

Try to hold this
pose for three to
five breaths.

Feel your two middle
fingers reaching away
from each other.

Broaden collarbones,
please.

Make sure this knee
is over this foot.

Use your inner thigh
muscles to support your leg.

79

extended side angle

Try to hold this
pose for three to
five breaths.

Palm faces down.

Turn ribcage toward
the ceiling. Look up
under your armpit.

Feel one long line of
energy from heel all the
way through fingertips.

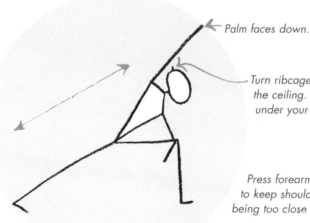

Press forearm into thigh
to keep shoulder from
being too close to your ear.

80

triangle pose

You can place your hand on the floor behind you or try putting a block or dictionary under your fingertips. You can also move your hand higher up your shin, even to just below the knee.

Try to hold this pose for three to five breaths.

Extend the crown of your head away from your tailbone.

Can you feel the air moving in and out of your lungs?

Make sure the inner and outer parts of the foot have equal weight.

Reach down into the earth with this leg.

81

warrior two

Try to hold this pose for three to five breaths.

Feel your two middle fingers reaching away from each other.

Keep your spine vertical.

Make sure this knee is over this foot.

82

cartwheel

Circle your back arm up and over, then place both arms on the floor on either side of your front foot.

Inhale.

plank pose

Hold inhale from cartwheel.

Keep arms and legs straight.

Extend energy out through your heels.

Slightly tone your belly to support the spine.

Keep wrists below shoulders.

four limbs pose

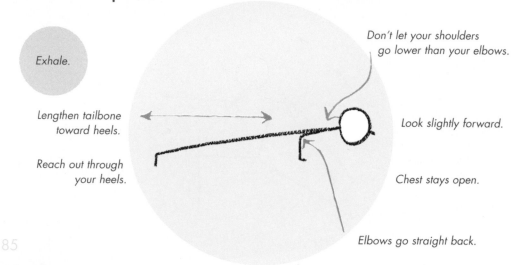

Exhale.

Don't let your shoulders go lower than your elbows.

Lengthen tailbone toward heels.

Look slightly forward.

Reach out through your heels.

Chest stays open.

Elbows go straight back.

85

upward dog

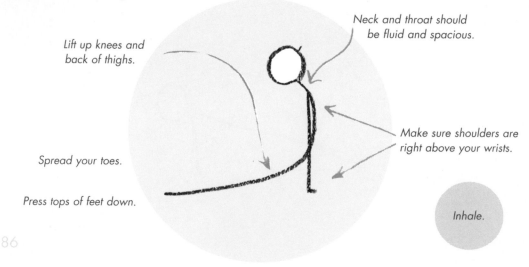

Lift up knees and back of thighs.

Neck and throat should be fluid and spacious.

Make sure shoulders are right above your wrists.

Spread your toes.

Press tops of feet down.

Inhale.

86

downward dog

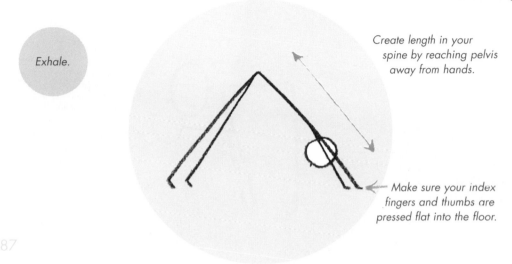

Exhale.

Create length in your spine by reaching pelvis away from hands.

Make sure your index fingers and thumbs are pressed flat into the floor.

87

jumping forward from downward dog

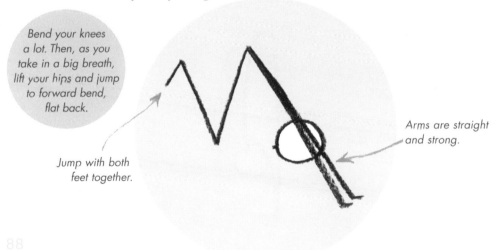

Bend your knees a lot. Then, as you take in a big breath, lift your hips and jump to forward bend, flat back.

Jump with both feet together.

Arms are straight and strong.

88

forward bend, flat back

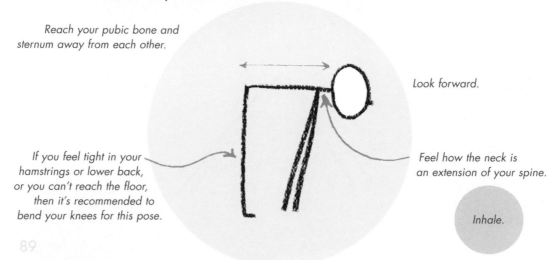

Reach your pubic bone and sternum away from each other.

Look forward.

If you feel tight in your hamstrings or lower back, or you can't reach the floor, then it's recommended to bend your knees for this pose.

Feel how the neck is an extension of your spine.

Inhale.

89

standing forward bend

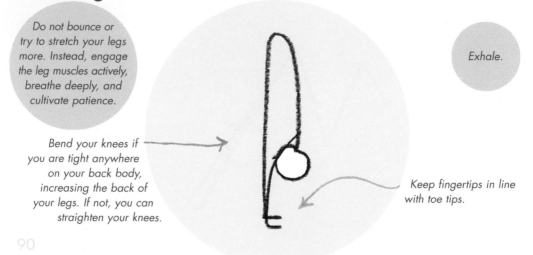

Do not bounce or try to stretch your legs more. Instead, engage the leg muscles actively, breathe deeply, and cultivate patience.

Exhale.

Bend your knees if you are tight anywhere on your back body, increasing the back of your legs. If not, you can straighten your knees.

Keep fingertips in line with toe tips.

90

reverse swan dive

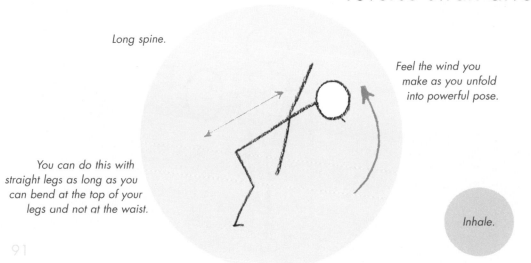

Long spine.

Feel the wind you make as you unfold into powerful pose.

You can do this with straight legs as long as you can bend at the top of your legs and not at the waist.

Inhale.

91

powerful pose

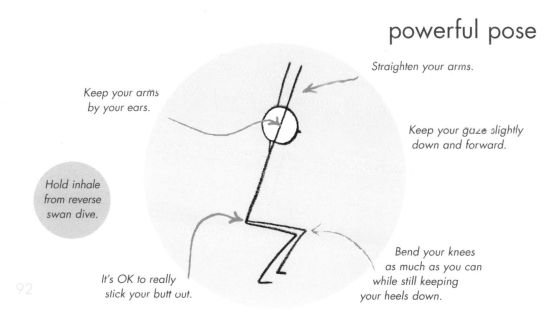

Straighten your arms.

Keep your arms by your ears.

Keep your gaze slightly down and forward.

Hold inhale from reverse swan dive.

It's OK to really stick your butt out.

Bend your knees as much as you can while still keeping your heels down.

92

mountain pose

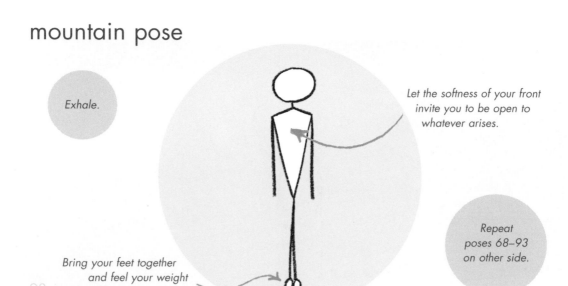

Exhale.

Let the softness of your front invite you to be open to whatever arises.

Bring your feet together and feel your weight dropping to the earth.

Repeat poses 68–93 on other side.

93

tree pose with side bend preparation

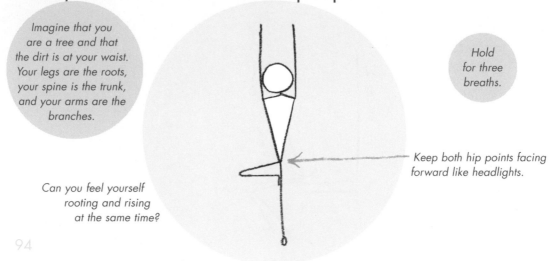

Imagine that you are a tree and that the dirt is at your waist. Your legs are the roots, your spine is the trunk, and your arms are the branches.

Hold for three breaths.

Keep both hip points facing forward like headlights.

Can you feel yourself rooting and rising at the same time?

94

tree pose with side bend

Reach out through your fingers and even the spaces between the fingers.

Look straight ahead. What can you see?

Lightly touch the knee.

Try to keep your hips pointing forward evenly.

Hold for three breaths.

Repeat poses 94–95 on other side.

95

forearm stand preparation

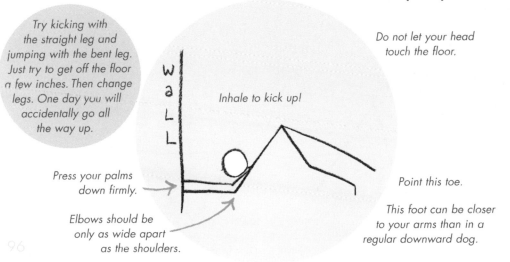

Try kicking with the straight leg and jumping with the bent leg. Just try to get off the floor a few inches. Then change legs. One day you will accidentally go all the way up.

Do not let your head touch the floor.

WaLL

Inhale to kick up!

Press your palms down firmly.

Elbows should be only as wide apart as the shoulders.

Point this toe.

This foot can be closer to your arms than in a regular downward dog.

96

forearm stand

Try to stay up here for three to five breaths. Don't forget to breathe!

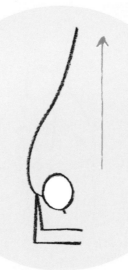

Reach up strongly with your tailbone; send energy up through inner thighs and inner heels.

Soften your front ribs and feel your breath in your back.

Keep your palms flat and in line with your elbows and shoulders.

97

headstand preparation

Place the top of your head on the floor, right behind your fist. Do not put your head in your hands.

Elbows should be as wide apart as shoulders, no wider.

Keep lifting up here.

Keep your neck long.

Reach your shoulders up toward your waist.

Make sure you are using your arm strength here so not all your weight is on your head.

Eventually you can straighten one leg with the other knee bent into your chest.

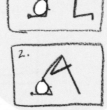

VARIATIONS

1.

2.

98

120

headstand, knees bent at wall

You can rest your hips
and your feet on the wall.

W
A
L
L

Gaze straight ahead.
Try to breathe evenly
and deeply and smoothly.

After five breaths,
come down
and rest.

99

Keep lifting your biceps,
triceps, and shoulders.

headstand

Draw your legs together and extend
up through your toes and heels.

The headstand is one of the
most beneficial poses in yoga.
But it takes a lot of strength
and confidence. Take
it one step at a time.

Move front ribs and
waist into your back.

Press down with forearms,
up with upper arms.

Very slowly, over a period
of many weeks or even
months or years, try to work
up to a ten-breath-long headstand.

100

child's pose

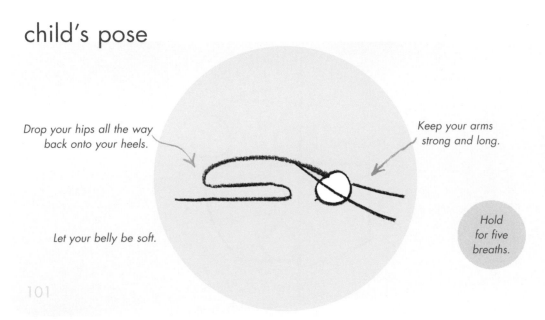

Drop your hips all the way back onto your heels.

Keep your arms strong and long.

Let your belly be soft.

Hold for five breaths.

101

locust pose

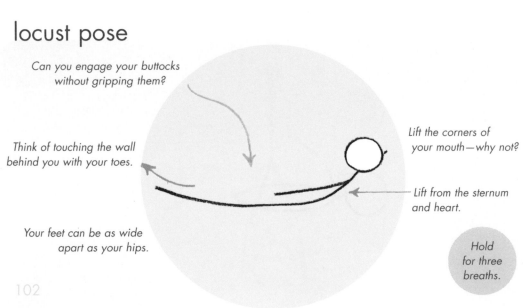

Can you engage your buttocks without gripping them?

Think of touching the wall behind you with your toes.

Lift the corners of your mouth—why not?

Lift from the sternum and heart.

Your feet can be as wide apart as your hips.

Hold for three breaths.

102

bow pose

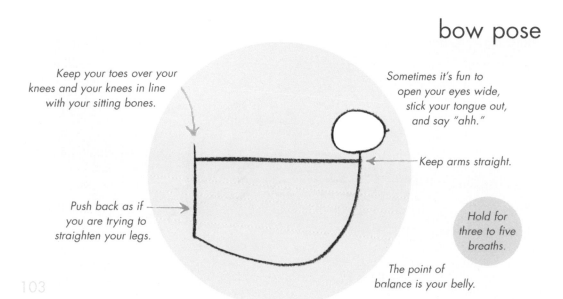

Keep your toes over your knees and your knees in line with your sitting bones.

Sometimes it's fun to open your eyes wide, stick your tongue out, and say "ahh."

Keep arms straight.

Push back as if you are trying to straighten your legs.

Hold for three to five breaths.

The point of balance is your belly.

103

half wheel

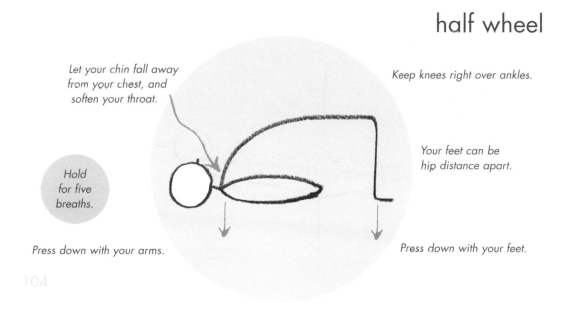

Let your chin fall away from your chest, and soften your throat.

Keep knees right over ankles.

Your feet can be hip distance apart.

Hold for five breaths.

Press down with your arms.

Press down with your feet.

104

wheel

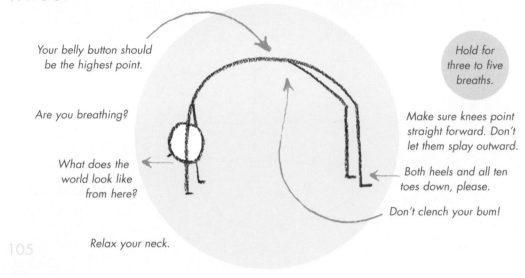

Your belly button should
be the highest point.

Are you breathing?

What does the
world look like
from here?

Relax your neck.

*Hold for
three to five
breaths.*

Make sure knees point
straight forward. Don't
let them splay outward.

Both heels and all ten
toes down, please.

Don't clench your bum!

windshield wipers

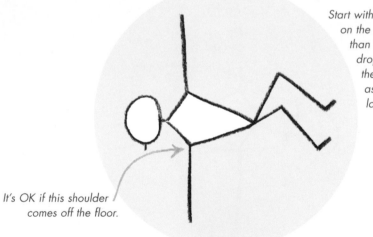

Start with your feet flat
on the floor, slightly wider
than your hips, then gently
drop them to one side,
then the other, as often
as you'd like for as
long as you'd like.

It's OK if this shoulder
comes off the floor.

right leg up lying on back, then left

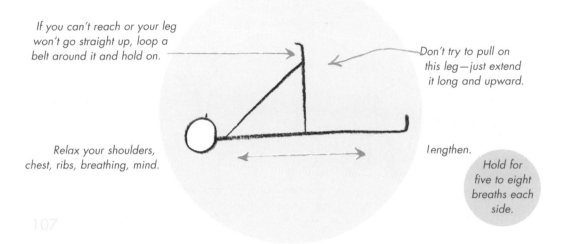

If you can't reach or your leg won't go straight up, loop a belt around it and hold on.

Don't try to pull on this leg—just extend it long and upward.

Relax your shoulders, chest, ribs, breathing, mind.

lengthen.

Hold for five to eight breaths each side.

107

straight leg supine twist

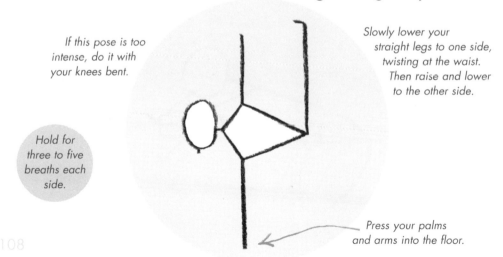

If this pose is too intense, do it with your knees bent.

Slowly lower your straight legs to one side, twisting at the waist. Then raise and lower to the other side.

Hold for three to five breaths each side.

Press your palms and arms into the floor.

108

cobbler's pose

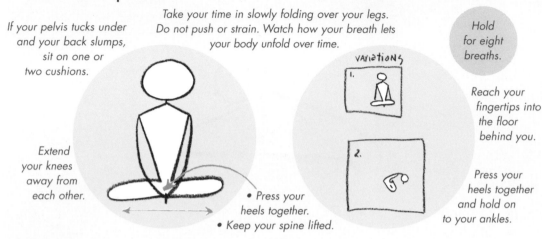

If your pelvis tucks under and your back slumps, sit on one or two cushions.

Take your time in slowly folding over your legs. Do not push or strain. Watch how your breath lets your body unfold over time.

Hold for eight breaths.

Extend your knees away from each other.

- Press your heels together.
- Keep your spine lifted.

VARIATIONS
1.
2.

Reach your fingertips into the floor behind you.

Press your heels together and hold on to your ankles.

109

head to knee pose

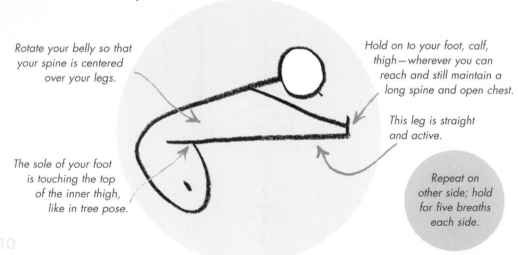

Rotate your belly so that your spine is centered over your legs.

Hold on to your foot, calf, thigh—wherever you can reach and still maintain a long spine and open chest.

This leg is straight and active.

The sole of your foot is touching the top of the inner thigh, like in tree pose.

Repeat on other side; hold for five breaths each side.

110

seated forward bend

This pose is said to be calming. Is that your experience?

Once again, hold on wherever you can reach and still keep your spine straight. Use a belt if you need to. Reach through your sternum, keeping the spine long as you fold over your legs.

Make sure your chest is open and your breath is free. You never want your pose to inhibit your heart and lung activity.

Hold for eight to ten breaths.

Flex your feet.

111

shoulder stand

You can stay here for five to ten breaths. Over time you can work up to five minutes.

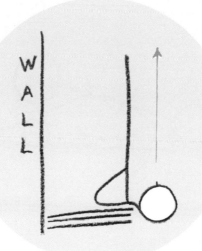

Zip your inner thighs together.

With Barbie doll feet, reach through the tips of your toes and relax your ankles.

Fold up three firm blankets and place them under your back.

Look up at your toes.

Try to relax your throat and let your chin and forehead fall away from your chest.

112

plow pose

You can stay here for five to ten breaths.

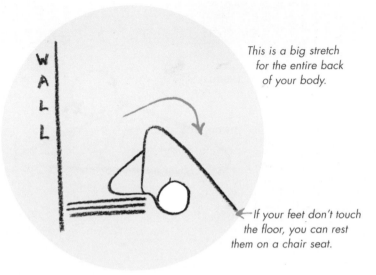

WALL

This is a big stretch for the entire back of your body.

←If your feet don't touch the floor, you can rest them on a chair seat.

113

corpse pose

You can also simply lie down flat on the ground and rest.

Stay here as long as you like.

Close your eyes. An eye pillow can be nice.

Feet should be about hip distance apart.

Turn your palms up.

A pillow under your knees can feel good to your lower back.

114

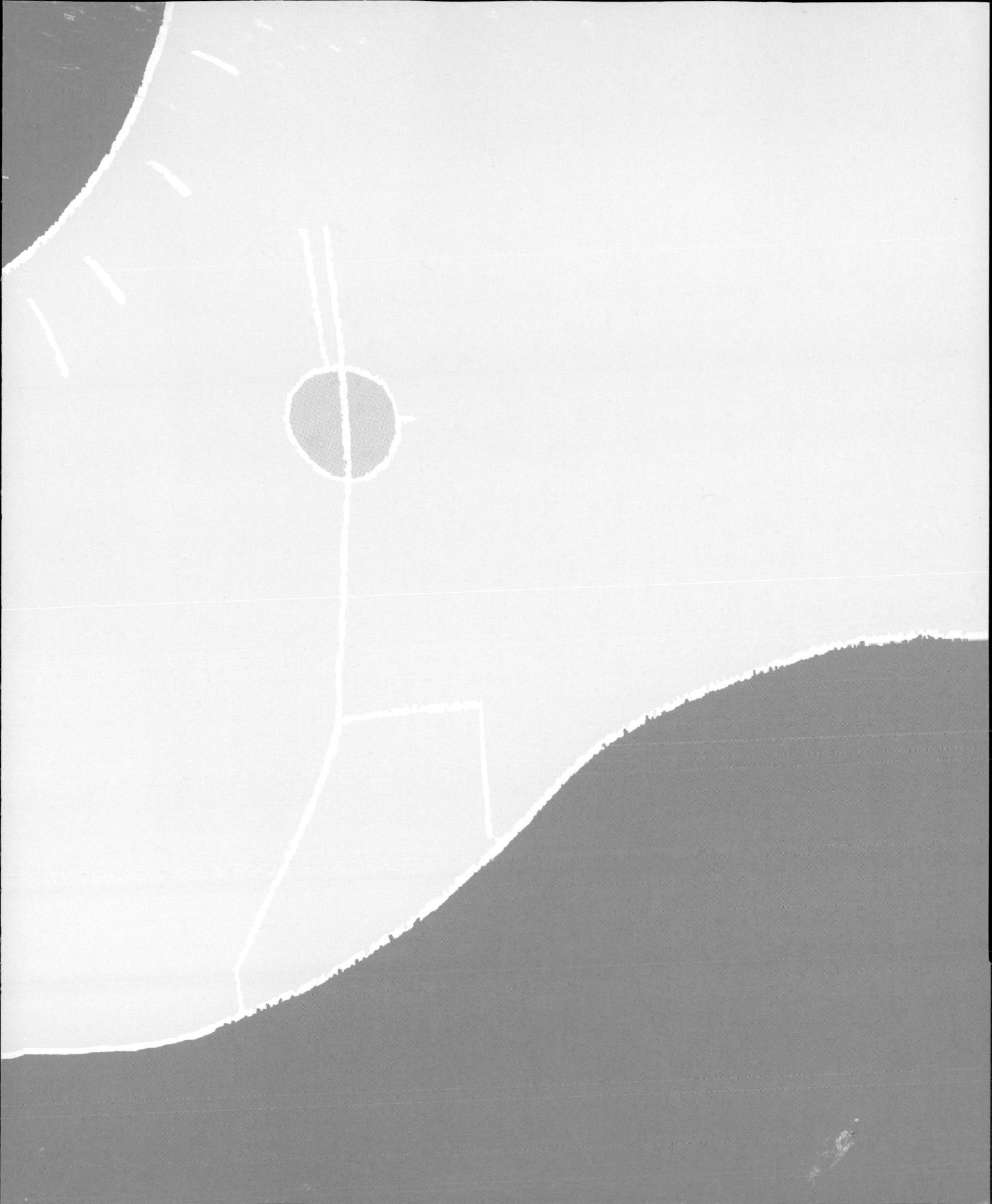

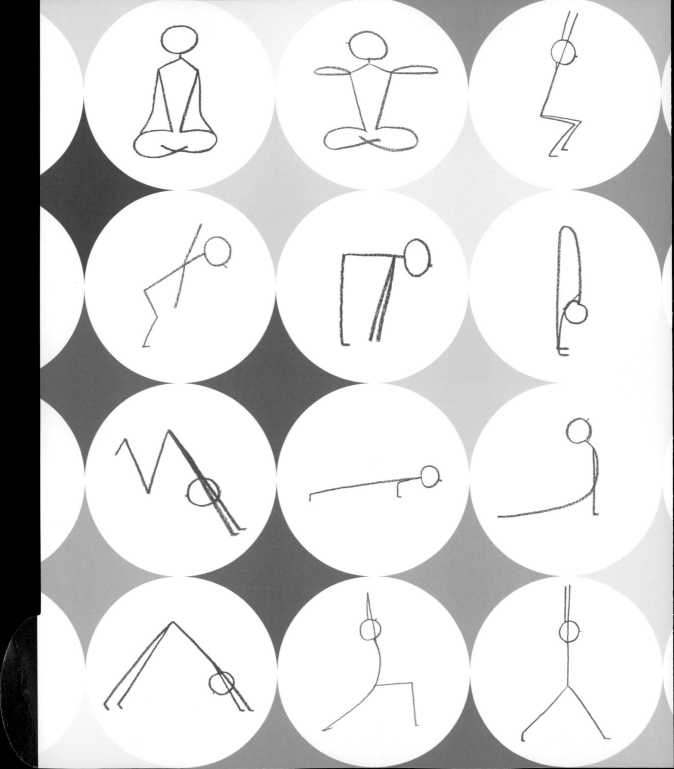

Ninety-Minute Session

So far your yoga has helped you connect to your body, breath, moods, thought patterns, family, environment, and even inner conflicts or resistance. All of this is yoga.

Yoga comes from the Sanskrit word *yuj*, which means to yoke or bind—in other words, union. But union with what? Some would say union with something outside our ordinary selves, a higher power or a divine energy. But isn't it possible that everything is inherently divine and the invitation of yoga is to cultivate the openness to connect with everything all the time?

Disconnecting from anything, whether it is something extraordinarily uplifting or just the stuff of everyday reality, is how we create our own discomfort. It's the choosing that's the problem. When we push away what we don't like, it just magnifies the irritation. But we also suffer when we try to hold on to what we like, because it will inevitably go away.

All of us experience constant change in every area of our life, some of these transitions more pleasant than others. Our bodies go through pregnancy, weight loss and gain, the natural aging process, and sickness, as well as wonderful phases of feeling great and being quite fit. Our families also morph as the kids leave home, our parents age, or maybe we get married for the first time, change jobs, or move to a new city. Changes beyond our control define our larger circle of activity, which includes heat waves and long winters, traffic jams and world politics.

Rolling along with these changes as they occur is union. In common parlance we might say, "Get with the program" or "Go with the flow." This doesn't mean that you throw your schedule out the window, but it does mean that we can learn to be flexible with how things unfold, and begin to cultivate a sense of relaxed wakefulness within not-knowing. Sounds good, but how do we practice that?

The first step toward connecting is to take stock of what is actually occurring from moment to moment. If you watch a yogini doing asana practice, at first glance it might appear that she is like a statue, completely static and doing nothing. But there is a lot of movement going on—heart beating, lungs breathing, blood circulating, and the mind producing thoughts. The yogini observes all this by continuously scanning her body, monitoring her breath, and witnessing the movement of her own mind.

Each asana is designed to create a specific pattern, which in turn creates a beneficial effect on our body, breath, and mind. But rather than going for a particular effect, our practice is to try to inhabit the structure of the asana with meditative awareness. The effects of the asanas will be slightly different each day, depending on what you ate for breakfast, what happened at work yesterday, and if your daughter is speaking to you today or not. Our task is to fully inhabit the pose by organizing our body into that physical shape or energy circuit and then, minute by minute, readjusting as our experience evolves.

This ninety-minute yoga session builds on all the previous sections and will give you plenty of opportunities to work with this approach. You can try out the following inner dialogue while doing your practice.

* Is my breath easy or obstructed? What adjustments can I make to free my breath?

* Is there evenness of effort throughout my body? Am I gripping in some places and drooping in others? What needs to happen to create equal awareness in all parts of my body?

* Can I try to be mindful from moment to moment, so that when things shift in my breathing pattern, or tension arises in one hip, or thoughts start to pull me off balance, I can reorganize to relate to that new situation? Can I do this over and over and over again?

* Do I have the same thought every time I do a certain thing, such as downward-facing dog? Handstand? Child's pose?

* Are my eyes and ears open?

With slight variations, these questions can be used as a map for developing awareness and flexibility anywhere, anytime. Developing skills for working with the constant shifts within your own body, breath, and mind is the first step toward negotiating the bigger picture of your life altogether.

We can start right now. Since this book is about time, take note of the time. What does it feel like? What is the feeling of this day? Month? Season? How does it smell? Do you feel the bright and early crispness of morning or the sleepy thickness following lunch? Ask these questions before, during, and after your practice. These questions might lead to more curiosity, which would lead to more connections, which would lead to more union, which would lead to more time to do yoga!

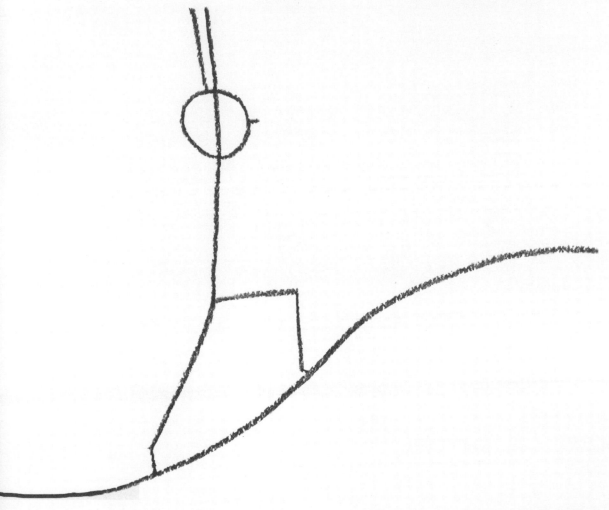

Ninety-Minute Session

1 sitting meditation: five minutes

2 breathing with twisting

3 cross legs, palms facing ceiling

4 curve back and press palms forward

5 arms up

6 side bend right

7 arms up

8 side bend left

9 arms up

10 twist right

11 arms up

12 twist left

13 arms up

14 backstroke arms

15 lift chest and stick out tongue

16 hands and knees

17 downward dog

18 hand walking meditation

19 forward bend

20 rounding up

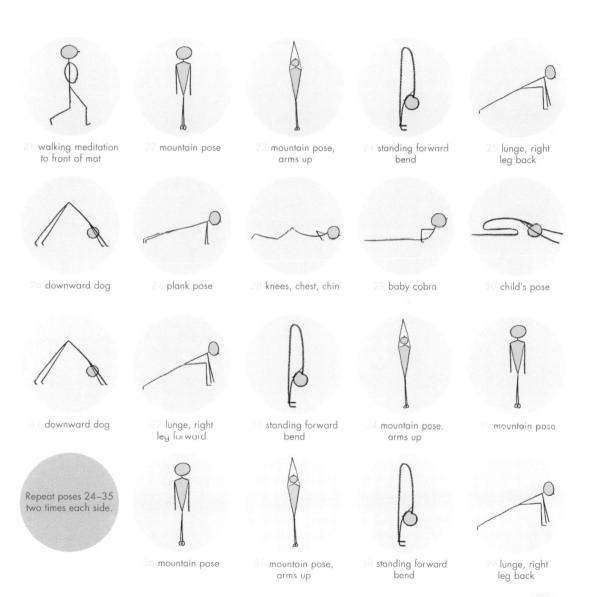

21 walking meditation to front of mat

22 mountain pose

23 mountain pose, arms up

24 standing forward bend

25 lunge, right leg back

26 downward dog

27 plank pose

28 knees, chest, chin

29 baby cobra

30 child's pose

31 downward dog

32 lunge, right leg forward

33 standing forward bend

34 mountain pose, arms up

35 mountain pose

Repeat poses 24–35 two times each side.

36 mountain pose

37 mountain pose, arms up

38 standing forward bend

39 lunge, right leg back

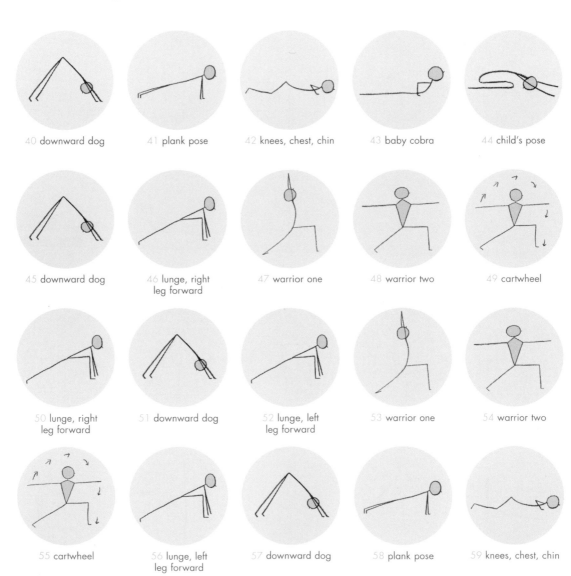

40 downward dog

41 plank pose

42 knees, chest, chin

43 baby cobra

44 child's pose

45 downward dog

46 lunge, right leg forward

47 warrior one

48 warrior two

49 cartwheel

50 lunge, right leg forward

51 downward dog

52 lunge, left leg forward

53 warrior one

54 warrior two

55 cartwheel

56 lunge, left leg forward

57 downward dog

58 plank pose

59 knees, chest, chin

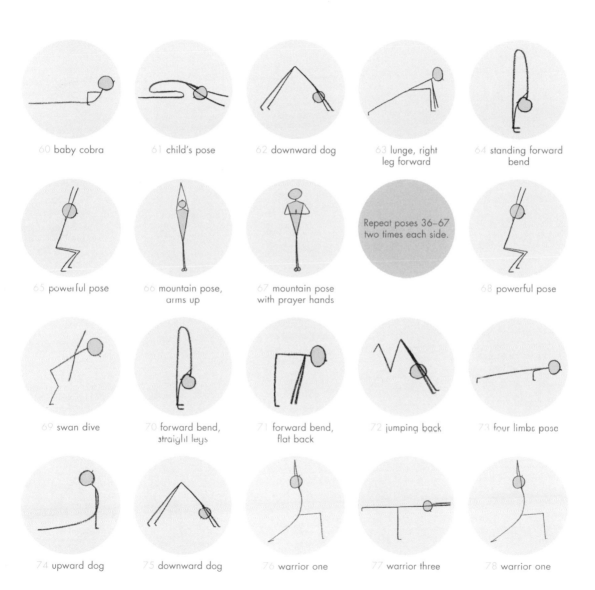

60 baby cobra

61 child's pose

62 downward dog

63 lunge, right
leg forward

64 standing forward
bend

65 powerful pose

66 mountain pose,
arms up

67 mountain pose
with prayer hands

Repeat poses 36–67
two times each side.

68 powerful pose

69 swan dive

70 forward bend,
straight legs

71 forward bend,
flat back

72 jumping back

73 four limbs pose

74 upward dog

75 downward dog

76 warrior one

77 warrior three

78 warrior one

Ninety-Minute Session

79 warrior two

80 extended side angle

81 triangle pose

82 warrior two

83 cartwheel

84 plank pose

85 four limbs pose

86 upward dog

87 downward dog

88 jumping forward from downward dog

89 forward bend, flat back

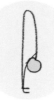

90 forward bend, straight legs

91 reverse swan dive

92 powerful pose

93 mountain pose

94 powerful pose

95 swan dive

96 standing forward bend

97 forward bend, flat back

98 jumping back

99 four limbs pose

100 upward dog

101 downward dog

102 warrior one, right leg forward

103 straight leg warrior one with straight arms

104 straight leg warrior, reverse prayer hands

105 forward bend

106 walk hands around

107 straddle forward bend

108 walk hands around

109 lunge, right foot forward

110 proposal pose

111 twist in proposal pose right

112 downward dog

113 plank pose

114 four limbs pose

115 upward dog

116 downward dog

Repeat poses 102–116 with left leg.

117 jumping forward

Ninety-Minute Session

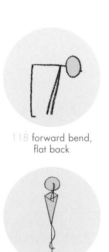

118 forward bend, flat back

119 standing forward bend

120 reverse swan dive

121 powerful pose

122 mountain pose

123 eagle pose

124 dancer pose

Repeat poses 123–124 on other side.

125 forearm stand

126 child's pose

127 L-shaped handstand preparation

128 L-shaped handstand walking up wall

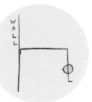

129 L-shaped handstand

130 handstand preparation

131 handstand

132 child's pose

133 downward dog

134 downward dog split

135 pigeon pose

136 pigeon half bow

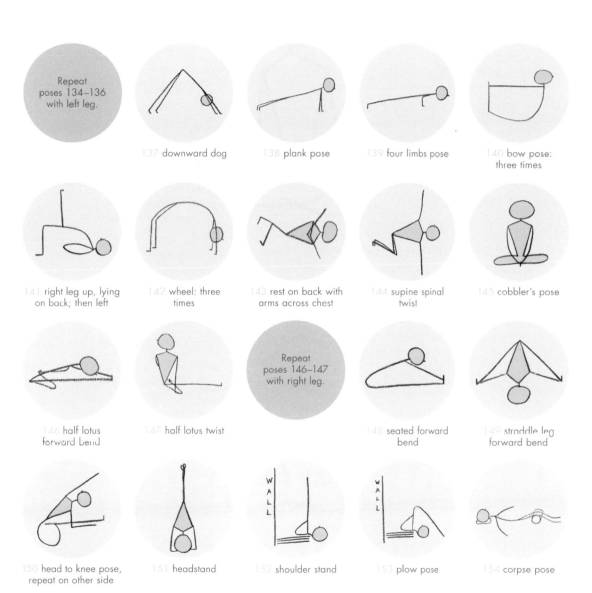

Repeat poses 134–136 with left leg.

137 downward dog

138 plank pose

139 four limbs pose

140 bow pose: three times

141 right leg up, lying on back; then left

142 wheel: three times

143 rest on back with arms across chest

144 supine spinal twist

145 cobbler's pose

146 half lotus forward bend

147 half lotus twist

Repeat poses 146–147 with right leg.

148 seated forward bend

149 straddle leg forward bend

150 head to knee pose, repeat on other side

151 headstand

152 shoulder stand

153 plow pose

154 corpse pose

sitting meditation: five minutes

You might not find it easy to sit like this at first, but as you begin to rest your mind, you may begin to experience a sense of ease.

Open the crown of your head up to heaven.

Soften your throat.

Feel your rib cage expand and contract as you breathe.

Cross your legs in a way that is comfortable for you. Try sitting on a cushion.

Let your sitting bones drop down into the earth.

1

breathing with twisting

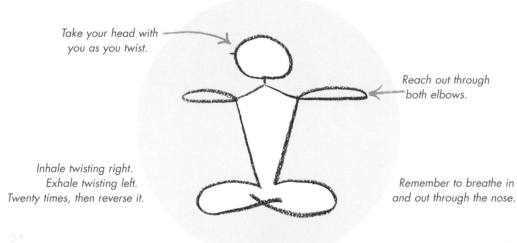

Take your head with you as you twist.

Reach out through both elbows.

Inhale twisting right.
Exhale twisting left.
Twenty times, then reverse it.

Remember to breathe in and out through the nose.

2*

*For poses 3–21, see pages 96–105. For poses 22–67, see pages 31–53. For poses 68–93, see pages 105–118.

powerful pose

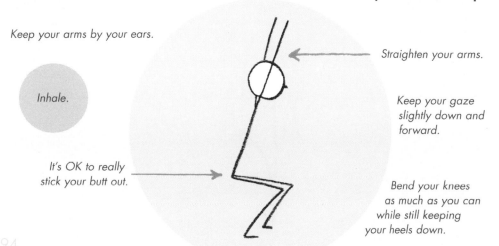

Keep your arms by your ears.

Straighten your arms.

Inhale.

Keep your gaze slightly down and forward.

It's OK to really stick your butt out.

Bend your knees as much as you can while still keeping your heels down.

94

swan dive

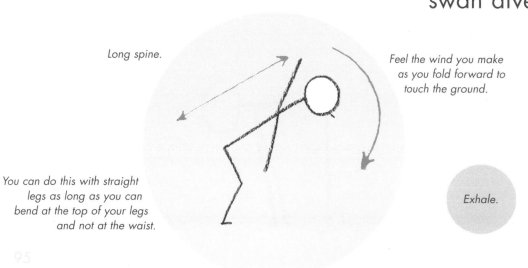

Long spine.

Feel the wind you make as you fold forward to touch the ground.

You can do this with straight legs as long as you can bend at the top of your legs and not at the waist.

Exhale.

95

standing forward bend

96

Hold exhale from swan dive.

Bend your knees if you are tight anywhere in back, including the back of your legs. If not, you can straighten your knees.

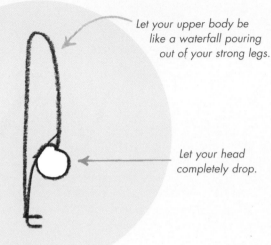

Let your upper body be like a waterfall pouring out of your strong legs.

Let your head completely drop.

forward bend, flat back

97

Reach your pubic bone and sternum away from each other.

If you feel tight in your hamstrings or lower back, or you can't reach the floor, then it's recommended to bend your knees for this pose.

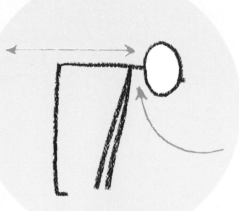

Inhale.

Look forward.

Feel how the neck is an extension of your spine.

jumping back

Exhale and inhale to four limbs pose.

Be sure to land with your knees bent.

Arms are straight and strong.

Jump with both feet together.

Jump into downward-facing dog, move into plank, bend elbows in four limbs pose.

98

four limbs pose

Exhale.

Don't let your shoulders go lower than your elbows.

Look slightly forward.

Lengthen tailbone toward heels.

Reach out through your heels.

Chest stays open.

Elbows go straight back.

99

upward dog

Inhale.

Lift up knees and back of thighs.

Spread your toes.

Press tops of feet down.

100

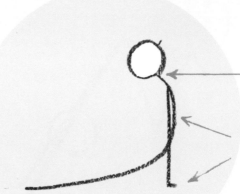

Neck and throat should be fluid and spacious.

Make sure shoulders are right above your wrists.

downward dog

Exhale.

101

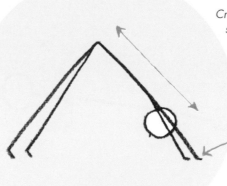

Create length in your spine by reaching pelvis away from hands.

Make sure your index fingers and thumbs are pressed flat into the floor.

warrior one, right leg forward

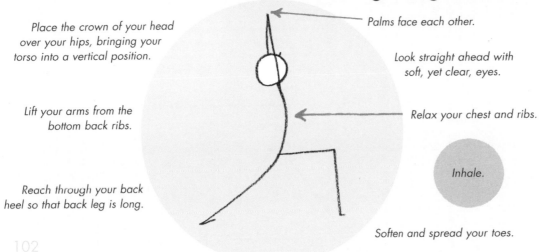

Place the crown of your head over your hips, bringing your torso into a vertical position.

Lift your arms from the bottom back ribs.

Reach through your back heel so that back leg is long.

Palms face each other.

Look straight ahead with soft, yet clear, eyes.

Relax your chest and ribs.

Inhale.

Soften and spread your toes.

102

straight leg warrior one with straight arms

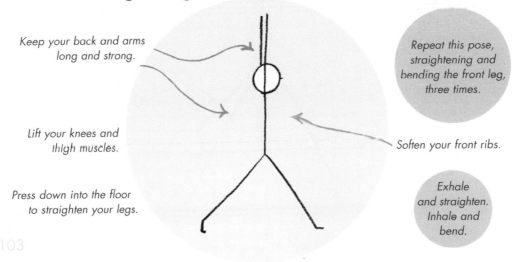

Keep your back and arms long and strong.

Lift your knees and thigh muscles.

Press down into the floor to straighten your legs.

Repeat this pose, straightening and bending the front leg, three times.

Soften your front ribs.

Exhale and straighten. Inhale and bend.

103

straight leg warrior, reverse prayer hands

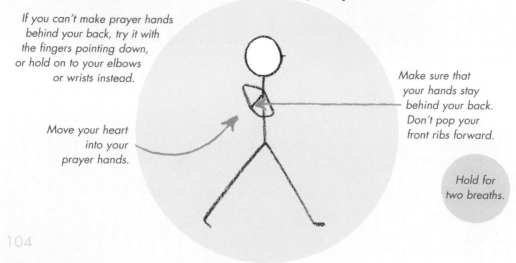

If you can't make prayer hands behind your back, try it with the fingers pointing down, or hold on to your elbows or wrists instead.

Make sure that your hands stay behind your back. Don't pop your front ribs forward.

Move your heart into your prayer hands.

Hold for two breaths.

104

forward bend

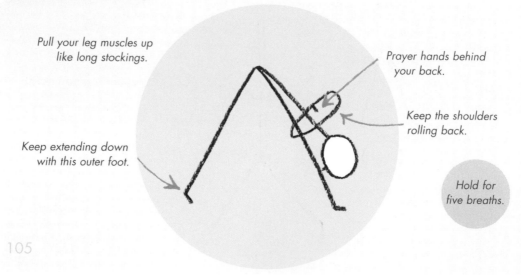

Pull your leg muscles up like long stockings.

Prayer hands behind your back.

Keep the shoulders rolling back.

Keep extending down with this outer foot.

Hold for five breaths.

105

walk hands around

Release your hands down to the floor and walk around to the right, taking the right foot around, too.

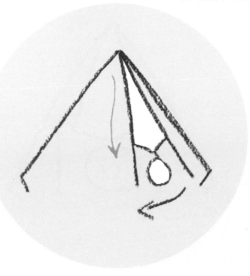

straddle forward bend

Sitting bones can blossom open and extend upward.

Strongly lift your leg muscles up your bones.

Fingertips are in line with toe tips.

Top of the head grazes the floor.

Keep your neck and shoulders broad.

Hold for five breaths.

VARiation

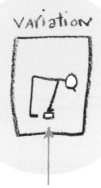

You can place your hands on a big book or the seat of a chair or on a table top.

walk hands around

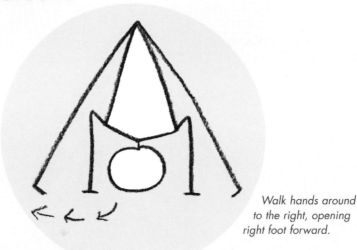

Walk hands around
to the right, opening
right foot forward.

108

lunge, right foot forward

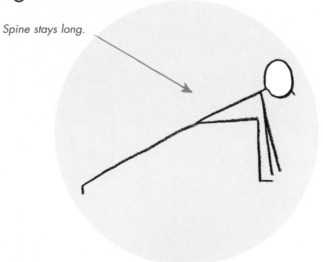

Spine stays long.

Inhale.

109

proposal pose

Let every finger be awake!

Lift your back ribs up!

Press the top of
your foot down to help
yourself feel grounded.

110

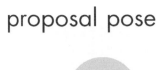

Exhale and
then inhale.

Let your front ribs
soften down.

Make sure this knee is
directly over the ankle.

Spread your toes wide.

twist in proposal pose right

Reach the elbows away from
each other while pressing
the hands together.

Lengthen your spine.

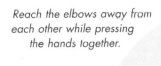

111

If this hurts your knee,
put a blanket underneath.

Exhale to
twist. Hold for
three to five
breaths.

Hook your elbow or
shoulder on the outside
of the knee.

Make sure this knee
and toe are pointing
straight ahead.

downward dog

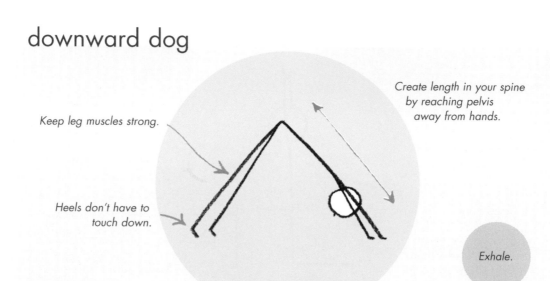

Create length in your spine
by reaching pelvis
away from hands.

Keep leg muscles strong.

Heels don't have to
touch down.

Exhale.

112

plank pose

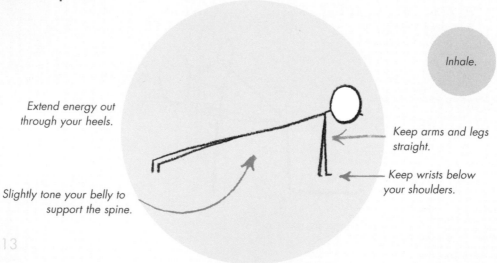

Inhale.

Extend energy out
through your heels.

Keep arms and legs
straight.

Keep wrists below
your shoulders.

Slightly tone your belly to
support the spine.

113

four limbs pose

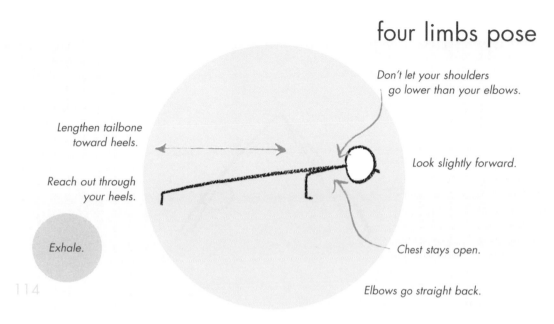

Don't let your shoulders go lower than your elbows.

Lengthen tailbone toward heels.

Look slightly forward.

Reach out through your heels.

Exhale.

Chest stays open.

114

Elbows go straight back.

upward dog

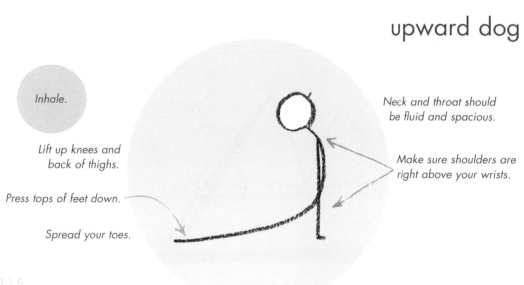

Inhale.

Neck and throat should be fluid and spacious.

Lift up knees and back of thighs.

Make sure shoulders are right above your wrists.

Press tops of feet down.

Spread your toes.

115

downward dog

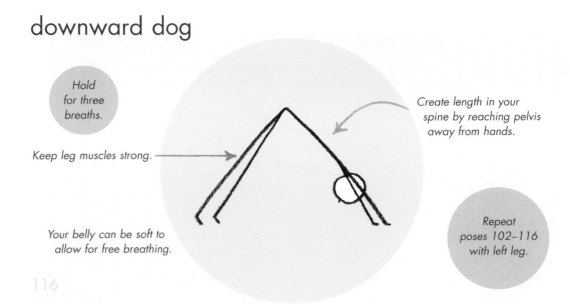

Hold for three breaths.

Keep leg muscles strong.

Create length in your spine by reaching pelvis away from hands.

Your belly can be soft to allow for free breathing.

Repeat poses 102–116 with left leg.

116

jumping forward

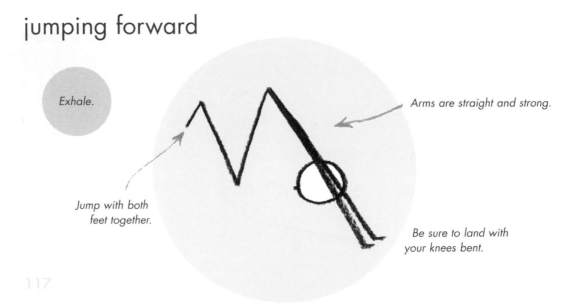

Exhale.

Arms are straight and strong.

Jump with both feet together.

Be sure to land with your knees bent.

117

forward bend, flat back

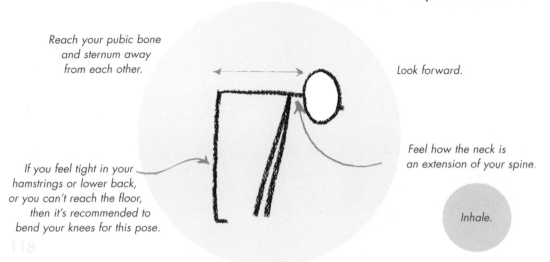

Reach your pubic bone and sternum away from each other.

Look forward.

If you feel tight in your hamstrings or lower back, or you can't reach the floor, then it's recommended to bend your knees for this pose.

Feel how the neck is an extension of your spine.

Inhale.

118

standing forward bend

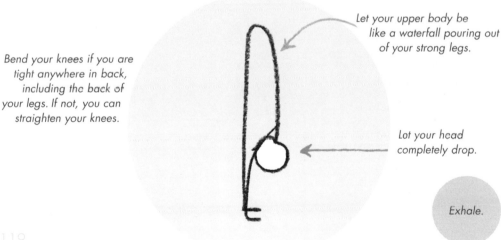

Let your upper body be like a waterfall pouring out of your strong legs.

Bend your knees if you are tight anywhere in back, including the back of your legs. If not, you can straighten your knees.

Let your head completely drop.

Exhale.

119

reverse swan dive

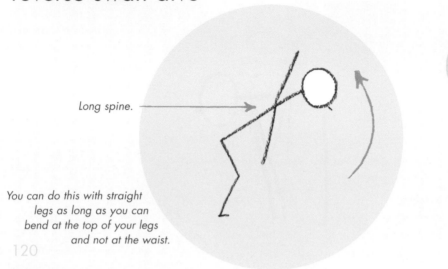

Long spine.

Inhale.

You can do this with straight legs as long as you can bend at the top of your legs and not at the waist.

120

powerful pose

Keep your arms by your ears.

Straighten your arms.

Hold inhale from reverse swan dive.

Keep your gaze slightly down and forward.

It's OK to really stick your butt out.

Bend your knees as much as you can while still keeping your heels down.

121

mountain pose

Hold
for three
breaths.

Let the softness of your front
invite you to be open to
whatever arises.

Bring your feet together
and feel your weight
dropping to the earth.

122

eagle pose

Place one upper arm over the
other, then cross your wrists and
press your palms together.
If you can't touch your
palms together, don't cross
your wrists, but simply
touch the backs of your
hands together.

Let your gaze be panoramic. Even
see out the back of your head.

The arm that wraps on top
should be the opposite
of the leg that is on top.

Even though this leg looks
straight here, in real life,
keep the standing leg as
bent as possible.

Wrap your leg once
way up high, then again
around the calf. One wrap
is also fine, or you can
put the toe on the floor.

Hold
for five
breaths.

123

dancer pose

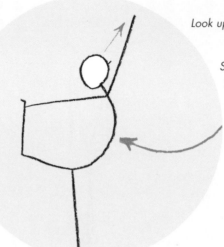

Press your ankle away
from your chest.

Look up at your hand.

Soften behind
your heart.

Make sure your knee
points back, not out to
the side.

Tone your belly slightly.

Repeat
poses 123–124
on other side; hold
for three to five
breaths on each
side.

Firm this leg up, as you
do in mountain pose.

124

forearm stand

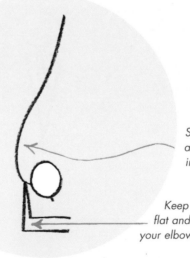

Reach up strongly with
your tailbone; send energy
up through inner thighs
and inner heels.

Try to stay
up here for three
to five breaths.
Don't forget to
breathe!

Soften your front ribs
and feel your breath
in your back.

Keep your palms
flat and in line with
your elbows and shoulders.

125

child's pose

Drop your hips all the way back onto your heels.

Keep your arms strong and long.

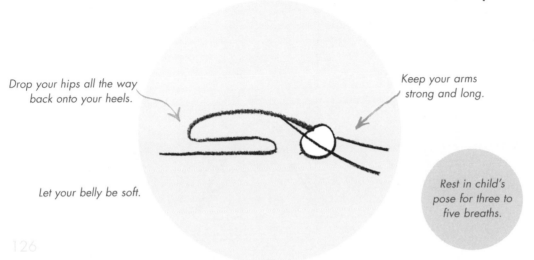

Let your belly be soft.

Rest in child's pose for three to five breaths.

126

L-shaped handstand preparation

Be precise with this set-up.

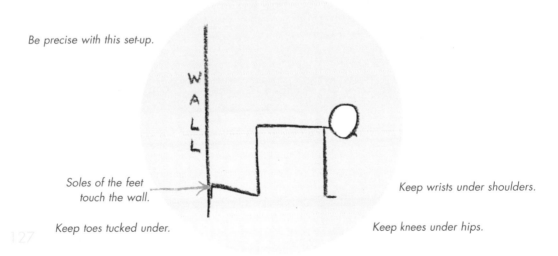

WALL

Soles of the feet touch the wall.

Keep toes tucked under.

Keep wrists under shoulders.

Keep knees under hips.

127

L-shaped handstand walking up wall

From the set-up, straighten your legs into downward dog at the wall. Begin to walk your feet up the wall.

W
A
L
L

Lengthen in the shoulder area.

You can take a small step and put both feet on the molding, if you have one.

Do not move your hands away from the wall, even though it feels like you should.

L-shaped handstand

Try to stay here for three breaths. Gradually increase to eight breaths.

W
A
L
L

Don't take your feet higher than your hips.

Reach up strongly with sitting bones.

Keep your legs straight by pushing your feet into the wall.

Keep your arms straight by pushing down.

handstand preparation

If you are scared, take your time. Make small hops. It's normal and smart to be cautious about being upside down.

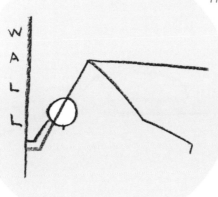

Practice kicking and jumping, just like in the forearm stand. Don't worry about getting up—you will get there eventually.

Look at a spot between your hands.

handstand

Extend through the balls of your feet. Keep a sense of space in your ankles. (Have Barbie doll feet.)

Try to work up to standing on your hands for three to five breaths.

Practice this at the wall. To balance, place your feet on the wall with your fingertips about six inches from the wall. Squeeze your thighs together and keep your arms straight by pushing down.

child's pose

Drop your hips all the way back onto your heels.

Let your belly be soft.

Hold for five breaths.

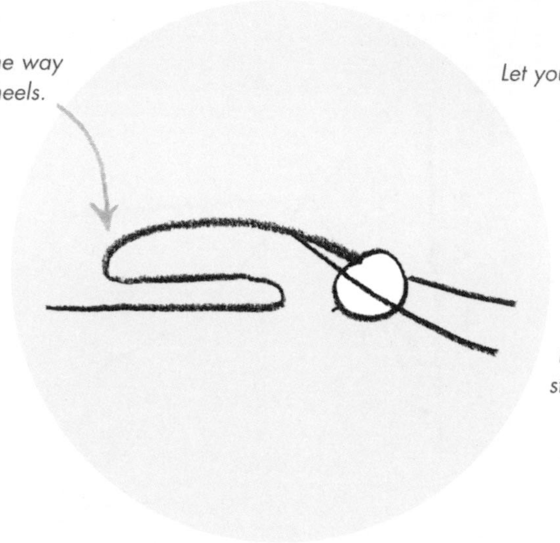

Keep your arms strong and long.

132

downward dog

Hold this downward-facing dog for three to five breaths. A breath means one complete inhale and exhale.

Create length in your spine by reaching pelvis away from hands.

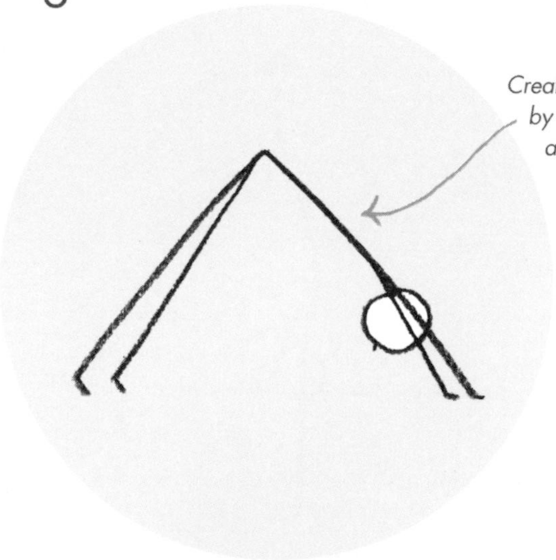

133

downward dog split

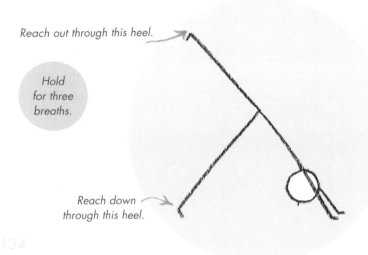

Reach out through this heel.

Can you make space between your ribs and hips?

Hold for three breaths.

Reach down through this heel.

Try not to dip either shoulder or either hip.

pigeon pose

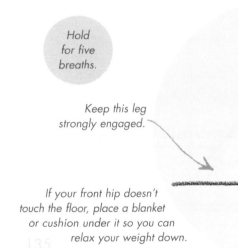

Hold for five breaths.

Keep this leg strongly engaged.

Chest faces forward.

Breathe deeply.

If your front hip doesn't touch the floor, place a blanket or cushion under it so you can relax your weight down.

This front knee can be slightly to the side. The foot can be close in to pelvis, but don't sit on it.

pigeon half bow

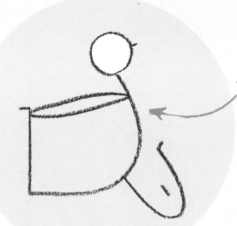

Reach your foot and your chest away from each other.

Ah . . . a yummy chest opener—breathe deeply.

Loop a belt around your ankle if you can't reach it.

Hold for three to five breaths.

136

downward dog

Leg muscles are strong.

Exhale.

Your belly can be soft to allow for free breathing.

Repeat poses 134–136 with left leg.

137

plank pose

Inhale.

Keep arms and legs straight.

Extend energy out through your heels.

Slightly tone your belly to support the spine.

Keep wrists below your shoulders.

four limbs pose

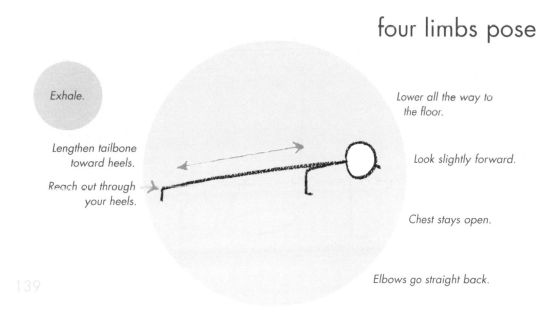

Exhale.

Lower all the way to the floor.

Lengthen tailbone toward heels.

Reach out through your heels.

Look slightly forward.

Chest stays open.

Elbows go straight back.

bow pose: three times

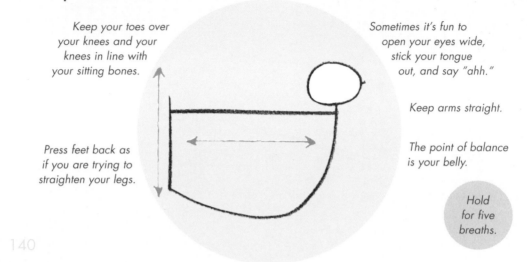

Keep your toes over your knees and your knees in line with your sitting bones.

Sometimes it's fun to open your eyes wide, stick your tongue out, and say "ahh."

Keep arms straight.

Press feet back as if you are trying to straighten your legs.

The point of balance is your belly.

Hold for five breaths.

140

right leg up, lying on back; then left

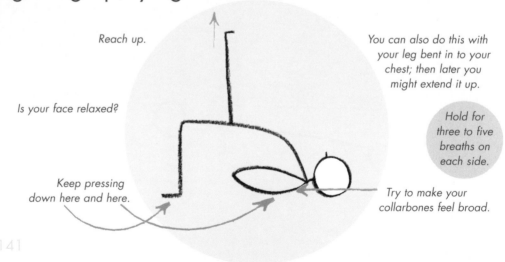

Reach up.

You can also do this with your leg bent in to your chest; then later you might extend it up.

Is your face relaxed?

Hold for three to five breaths on each side.

Keep pressing down here and here.

Try to make your collarbones feel broad.

141

wheel: three times

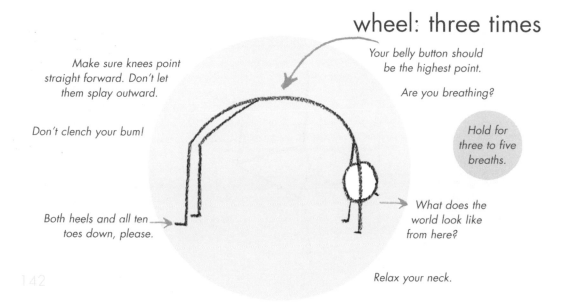

Make sure knees point straight forward. Don't let them splay outward.

Your belly button should be the highest point.

Are you breathing?

Don't clench your bum!

Hold for three to five breaths.

Both heels and all ten toes down, please.

What does the world look like from here?

Relax your neck.

142

rest on back with arms across chest

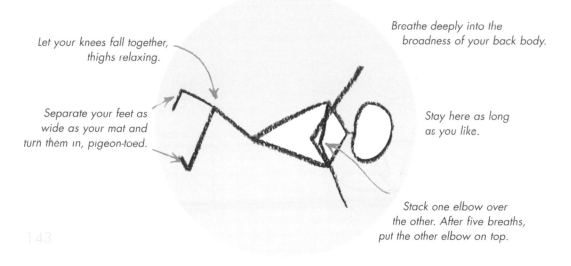

Let your knees fall together, thighs relaxing.

Breathe deeply into the broadness of your back body.

Separate your feet as wide as your mat and turn them in, pigeon-toed.

Stay here as long as you like.

Stack one elbow over the other. After five breaths, put the other elbow on top.

143

supine spinal twist

Relax your neck
and throat.

It's OK if you can't stack
the top knee directly over
the bottom one.

Release your weight
into the floor.

Repeat on other
side; hold for three
to five breaths on
each side.

Turn the palms up.

cobbler's pose

If your pelvis tucks under
and your back slumps,
sit on one or
two cushions.

Take your time in slowly folding over your legs.
Do not push or strain. Watch how your breath lets
your body unfold over time.

Hold
for ten
breaths.

VARIATIONS

1.

2.

Reach your
fingertips
into the floor
behind you.

Extend
your knees
away from
each other.

• Press your
heels together.
• Keep your spine lifted.

Press your
heels together
and hold on to
your ankles.

half lotus forward bend

From cobbler's pose, bring your left knee up and extend your left leg along the floor. Place your hands underneath your right shin. Then lift your right ankle up and place it in your left groin. Take a breath in. As you exhale, fold forward.

This is your left arm. Hold your foot, ankle, or chin—wherever you can reach.

Hold for five breaths.

This is your right hand behind your back, holding your right toe.

Still keep your spine long and leg straight.

Keep your sitting bones grounded.

If you feel any twinge in your right knee, do head to knee pose instead.

146

half lotus twist

Hold for five breaths.

This is your right hand holding your right ankle. Try to catch your foot, but if you can't reach it, use a belt or towel.

Spin the belly around.

This is your right arm.

Repeat poses 146–147 with right leg.

Flex your left wrist and tuck it under your thigh, palm down.

Left leg strong!

Right leg in half lotus.

147

seated forward bend

This pose is said to be calming. Is that your experience?

Once again, hold on wherever you can reach and still keep your spine straight. Use a belt if you need to. Reach through your sternum, keeping the spine long as you fold over your legs.

Make sure your chest is open and your breath is free. You never want your pose to inhibit your heart and lung activity.

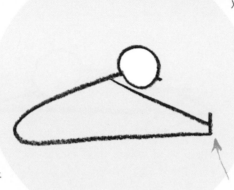

Hold for eight to ten breaths.

Flex your feet.

148

straddle leg forward bend

If your pelvis tucks under and your back slumps, sit on one or two cushions.

Take your time in slowly folding over your legs. Do not push or strain. Watch how your breath lets your body unfold over time.

It takes quite a while for almost everybody to do this, so start here with your back straight, chest open, and fingertips on the floor slightly in front of you.

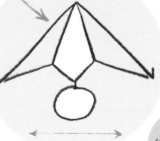

Extend your knees away from each other.

variations

1.

2.

Hold for five to eight breaths.

Eventually you may get your forearms down.

149

head to knee pose

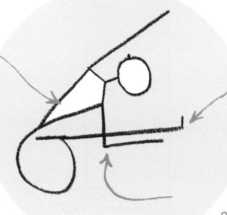

Rotate your belly up.

Reach out through your heel.

Repeat this pose on other side; hold for five breaths on each side.

Press your elbow, forearm, and palm down to lift up out of the shoulder and create length along the bottom ribs.

150

headstand

Draw your legs together and extend up through your toes and heels.

The headstand is one of the most beneficial poses in yoga. But it takes a lot of strength and confidence. Take it one step at a time.

Move front ribs and waist into your back.

Press down with forearms, up with upper arms.

Very slowly, over a period of many weeks or even months or years, try to work up to a ten-breath-long headstand.

151

shoulder stand

You can stay here for five to ten breaths. Over time you can work up to five minutes.

Zip your inner thighs together.

With Barbie doll feet, reach through the tips of your toes and relax your ankles.

Look up at your toes.

Try to relax your throat, and let your chin and forehead fall away from your chest.

Fold up three firm blankets and place them under your back.

WALL

You can substitute legs-up-the-wall pose, if you like.

152

plow pose

Hold for five breaths.

This is a big stretch for the entire back of your body.

WALL

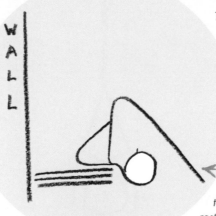

If your feet don't touch the floor, you can rest them on a chair seat.

153

corpse pose

154

You can also simply lie down flat on the ground and rest.

Stay here as long as you like.

Close your eyes. An eye pillow can be nice.

Feet should be about hip distance apart.

Turn your palms up.

A pillow under your knees can feel good to your lower back.

forward bending

twisting

backward bending

side bending

balancing

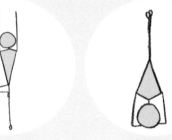

inverting

breath awareness

resting

meditation

Dedicating Your Practice

The benefits of our practice are both immediate and far-reaching, personal and universal, tangible and unspoken. Without even trying, over time you will probably begin to notice that the growing sense of presence, confidence, and connection that arises from your yoga practice radiates out to others.

You might also notice a feeling of appreciation at the end of your practice. A wonderful way to acknowledge this appreciation and share it with others is by dedicating the merits of your practice. If you would like to do this, take a moment to consciously recognize the effects of your practice today and share them with the rest of the world by saying this prayer at the end of your yoga session. This prayer is called "The Four Immeasurables," and it is a way to remind ourselves that although we will never meet them all, there are many, many beings in the world and we are all connected.

May all beings have happiness and the causes of happiness.

May all beings be free from suffering and the causes of suffering.

May all beings never be parted from freedom's true joy.

May all beings dwell in equanimity, free from attachment and aversion.

Glossary

Asana: This word refers to the physical postures of hatha yoga practice. It means "seat" or the part of your body that is touching the ground. For example, in the word *sirsasana, sirsa* is "head" and *asana* means "seat," so it means "put your head on the ground" or "headstand."

Breathing: Conscious manipulated breathing is an essential part of yoga and is traditionally called *pranayama. Prana* means "life force," and it can be found in air, water, earth, sunshine, humans, and animals. We can most easily experience it and control it through conscious manipulated breathing technique. *Ayama* means "extension," so *pranayama* is a series of breathing exercises designed to lengthen life as well as to improve its quality. Yogis say that each person has a predetermined number of breaths for his or her life, so the theory is that if you can learn to lengthen each breath, you will live longer.

Calm abiding: This term refers to turning to and resting in the mind's own natural state of peace.

Hatha: This often translates as "forceful" and refers to the energy and effort that is involved in asana practice. We often think of yoga as relaxing, but it takes strength of mind as well as muscle to hold your body in an asana for more than two seconds. This effort is part of the path to discovering spaciousness. Hatha yoga teaches us that rather than being aggressive, willpower can mean being wakeful, focused, and on the dot. This balance is also implied in the word *hatha. Ha* means "sun," which yoga philosophy considers to have masculine qualities of activity, heat, outward energy, and light. *Tha* means moon, which contains the feminine qualities of receptivity, coolness, turning inward, and darkness.

Householder: A householder is a practitioner of yoga or meditation who lives in the world with a home, family, and job, as opposed to a cave-dwelling ascetic yogi.

Mindfulness: Mindfulness is relaxed awareness of each moment.

Mudra: A physical seal, such as placing the thumb and first finger together, which creates a specific energetic circuit that will create a certain experience. For example, placing your palms flat on your thighs is called the mudra of calm abiding. You may feel that turning your palms down is like gently putting a lid on your overstimulated nervous system.

If you are sleepy while meditating, it is recommended that you use the cosmic mudra, which is palms turned up, fingers of one hand on top of the other, with your thumb tips lightly touching. This mudra should be held slightly above your lap, and if you start to fall asleep, your hands will drop and awaken you.

Some asanas, such as the shoulder stand, are also considered mudras.

OM: The sound of OM is created from four parts: A, U, M, and the silence after the sound. The silence is called the *turiya* and is said to include all the sounds of the universe. It can be felt as a vibration and reminds us that all the sounds we hear—our heartbeats, thunder, birds singing, even jackhammers—are all sound manifestations of the pulsation of the cosmos that moves through all of us all the time.

Prana: Life force or primordial energy that flows through all living beings. *Prana* can also be found in elements that create life, such as sunlight, water, and earth.

Savasana: This is one of the most important poses in yoga practice. It is translated as the "corpse pose" and is traditionally done at the end of every yoga class. It gives our bodies a chance to assimilate all the benefits of the more active poses, as well as a chance for our body temperatures to cool down after a vigorous practice. Although it seems that doing *savasana* is like taking a nap, it has the same dynamic as all yoga poses, which is a balance of wakefulness and relaxation. So although your body may be still, in *savasana* yogis are invited to watch their minds and remain alert, just as in meditation practice.

Shamatha: Traditional Tibetan Buddhist meditation technique that means "calm abiding" or "resting in peace." It is done with the eyes open, using the breath as a reference point for returning to and resting in the present moment. This method of one-pointed concentration leads to an increased ability to concentrate and is the ground for yoga practice and more advanced meditation techniques.

In walking meditation, *shamatha* is merged with *vipassana*, or a lifting of the eyes during which the meditator begins to experience a larger awareness of the environment in her consciousness.

Vinyasa: This refers to a flowing form of yoga in which asanas are strung together like beads on a necklace, and the string that connects them is the breath. It can be done slowly and spaciously or faster, giving each asana only one breath. This form generates heat, cultivates coordination and gracefulness, and reminds us that the transitions are just as important as the poses.

Yoga: Yoga is a state of being, a feeling of union with all that is. It is also a series of practices that includes codes of conduct, physical exercises, breathing exercises, and meditation.

Yogi: A male practitioner of yoga.

Yogini: A female practitioner of yoga.

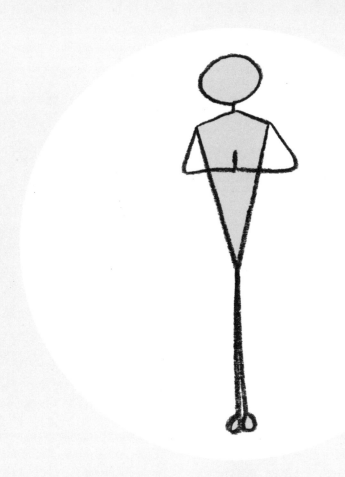